Books by Matthew Lowes

Spirituality

That Which is Before You (2020)
When You are Silent It Speaks (2021)
A Billion Fingers Point at the Moon (2022)
Lighting the Sacred Fire (2024)
Meditation (Coming in 2026)

Fiction

The End of All Things (2018)

Games

Elements of Chess (2012)
Dungeon Solitaire: Labyrinth of Souls (2016)
Dungeon Solitaire: Devil's Playground (2018)

LIGHTING THE SACRED FIRE

LIGHTING THE SACRED FIRE

MATTHEW LOWES

ENGAGING IN SPIRITUAL PRACTICE

Empty Press

2024

Lighting the Sacred Fire:
Engaging in Spiritual Practice
/ Matthew Lowes
ISBN 978-1-952073-06-9 (pbk.)

Typeset in
Minion Pro by Robert Slimbach
Source Sans pro by Paul D. Hunt

Empty Press

matthewlowes.com

Table of Contents

If you share with all beings the merit of a practice or positive action, that merit will last until you reach enlightenment, just as a drop of water that you put into the ocean will never dry up, for as long as the ocean remains.

But if you neglect to share the merit, it is like pouring a drop of water on a hot stone — it evaporates right away. Or it is like a seed that bears fruit once and then dies.

—Dilgo Khyentse Rinpoche, *The Heart of Compassion*

Spiritual practice is not just sitting and meditation. Practice is looking, thinking, touching, drinking, eating and talking. Every act, every breath, and every step can be practice and can help us to become more ourselves.

—Thich Nhat Hanh, "This Moment is Perfect"

Acknowledgements

Many thanks to all my teachers, students, friends, family, and loved ones. Thanks to all who read and commented on early drafts of this book. And thanks to all who read the books preceding this one. I am ever-grateful and deeply appreciate your contributions to this work. A very special thanks to Joel Morwood, Kaizen Taki, and Emily Bellinger.

LIGHTING THE SACRED FIRE

Introduction

Many teachings focus on conceptualizing the spiritual path, but without experience, receiving such teachings is like hearing about a distant land. It sounds great, but it's still far removed from our everyday life. If we imagine our spiritual lives as a journey, we don't get very far by just hearing stories or looking at picture books. Eventually we have to start walking, and spiritual practice is where the soles of your feet meet the dust of the road.

There's a difference between intellectual understanding and direct experience, between theory and real knowledge. To bridge this gap, we have to engage in practice, so that is our subject here.

This is the fourth book in a series addressing spirituality, awakening, and enlightenment. The first book includes an account of my awakening, and an overview of insights, teachings, and practices. The second book examines the whole of the spiritual journey, from beginning to end. The third book attempts to clear up any confusion and misconceptions arising from the ambiguous nature of language and spiritual discourse. And this book will examine the subject of practice in greater detail.

Each book stands on its own, but it makes some sense to approach them in order. Whether you have read the previous offerings or not, this book assumes you've already received some essential teachings and is meant to address the subject of practice only. Although a discussion about practice really isn't about enlightenment, it *is* about working with and removing obstacles that veil the truth. So in many ways, this is the most important discussion.

In the pages ahead, we'll look at the central role practice plays in the spiritual adventure. We'll explore the general structure of practice, illuminate the major paths and practices in greater detail, and discuss a range of related topics. Finally, we'll give some advice on how to handle persistent obstacles, road blocks, hang-ups, freak-outs, and difficulties.

Please note, this isn't a guidebook. I don't intend to give detailed instructions on particular practices, although some instruction is included as part of the discussion. For my instructions on practice, please see Part 4 of the first book in this series, *That Which is Before You,* or the next book in this series, which will provide a complete methodology for meditation. For ongoing instruction on practice, you're well advised to seek out a good teacher. For a detailed guidebook to a broad array of spiritual practices, my highest recommendation is Joel Morwood's book, *The Way of Selflessness.* I have never seen a more comprehensive guide written by someone who has walked the path and who knows where it leads.

Our purpose here is to better understand the landscape of spiritual practice, and to offer a commentary on the path that is both inspiring and helpful. So whatever practices you're interested in or happen to be doing, I hope this book will be a good companion on your path — and may that path lead to illumination, true happiness, and an end to suffering.

PART ONE

SACRED FIRE

Wherein we establish the role of practice on the spiritual path and outline its structure and elements.

1

LIGHTING THE SACRED FIRE

Fire has held a special place in people's lives for as long as humans have been humans. Fire touches upon the most practical daily endeavors of survival, and it reaches up to the most exalted visions, thoughts, and conceptions. From Vedic traditions going back 4000 years to the Paschal Candle lit on the Easter Vigil, sacred fire has been a symbol of humanity's connection to the divine.

As we warm ourselves by the fire, we sit at a hearth of life-sustaining heat. As we gather near a fire, the flames, sparks, and smoke reach up toward the mystery of the heavens — and if we follow them, so do our minds and hearts. Fire has become a symbol of life itself and our greatest spiritual endeavors.

Our traditions are filled with fire images. Agni, the Vedic fire god, carries prayers to the other gods. Prometheus delivered fire from the gods to mankind. God appeared to Moses as fire in the burning bush. The disciples of Christ were identified by flames that appeared above their heads. Fire is the flame behind the sacred heart. Fire is the luminous consciousness of the Buddhas. Fire is the warmth of the great spirit. Fire is the light of the cosmos. And so on.

Our languages are filled with fire metaphors. In the mind it burns as desire. In the body it burns as passion. In the heart it burns as longing. But fire also dispels evil and ignorance. It purifies, transforms and enlightens — so ultimately, it can burn as wisdom in the mind, as luminosity in the body, and as love in the heart.

When, in the course of our lives, we hear such a transformation is possible — that confusion can become wisdom, that anger can become clarity, that suffering can become peace, that ignorance can become enlightenment — a spark is kindled. When we hear this good news, a fire is lit, right in the midst of our lives. And this fire is the burning heart of our spiritual journey. This desire for the truth alone, this passion for reality laid bare, this longing for God, this sacred fire, is the engine of our inquiry, our prayer, and our practice.

Will to the Truth

After the sacred fire is lit, whether we know it or not, the spiritual journey begins in earnest. In many different ways, we will be drawn toward spiritual thoughts, things, books, teachings, and practices. But at the same time, we may feel more lost and confused than ever. Which direction do we go? What path do we follow? And now that we're seeking the truth and an end to suffering, our own suffering may actually become more noticeable and acute.

The plain fact is we don't know how to proceed, nor do we know where we're going. It's important to admit that. We may have some ideas according to what we've heard, read, or experienced, but we're not looking for an idea or memory. Our longing is for reality itself, not for concepts or particular experiences. Our determination is to discover the Truth. But, firmly planted in our experience of inhabiting a physical world as a separate body-mind, existing in time between an imagined birth and an imagined death, we have no direct knowledge of the truth we seek. We cannot even really imagine it.

So as we proceed on our journey, our greatest asset is not whatever knowledge we've accumulated, nor any skill we've developed, nor even our devotion or worldly compassion. All that can be helpful, of course, but our *greatest* asset is our will to the truth — our longing to discover what we really are, what the world really is, and what is really happening. The earnestness and tenacity with which we carry out this venture is critically important.

Without a will to the truth, it's far too easy to become complacent in life. We may hole up in some reasonably comfortable samsaric space and not risk pressing ahead on our spiritual quest. We may convince ourselves we can be satisfied with some extraordinary but temporary glimpses beyond our mind. We may rest on the laurels of attaining some stature as a person, a meditator, a monk, or a teacher.

But deep down, we know any worldly satisfaction we enjoy is temporary, and our longing to directly experience the truth of reality persists. Our longing to discover what we really are cannot be satisfied by anything less than full realization. And so, as seekers and practitioners, we should let this will to the truth come to surface, guide our lives, and throw wood onto the fire.

The Place of Practice

Today more than ever, many teachings are available, from the treasury of spiritual books and sacred texts to the wealth of teachers we can hear on recordings and live-streams. In a way, accessing the teachings of spiritual wisdom has never been easier. But the path itself is as difficult as ever. Why is that?

For a few people, who through experience, suffering, and practice, have already brought themselves to the edge of awakening, a gesture toward the truth is all that's needed. Sometimes just being in the presence of one who has realized is enough. Such seekers are like bits of burnt charcoal. In fact, they are at the cusp of enlightenment already. But others are like green wood, and just hearing the teaching is not enough. For this reason, we have a vast panoply of spiritual practices to set us on the path and help bring us to the doorstep of awakening.

We may have heard stories of spontaneous awakenings and teachings that declare no practice is necessary, but that's not a complete picture. Such stories and teachings can address particular mental obstacles, such as attachment to practice, feelings of unworthiness, or belief that enlightenment is far off or requires endless work. Of course, when it happens, awakening is spontaneous, and for the realized being no practice is necessary. But usually, if not always, awakening has followed some kind effort and practice, even if it's just looking inward and seeking the truth.

By and large, it's not enough to hear some teachings or read a few books. That's significant, but what we really need is to put good teachings into practice. If we read about how great meditation is but don't meditate, are we sincere in putting the teachings into practice? If we hear about inquiry, but don't earnestly inquire, can we expect realization? If we go to church or temple, but don't practice embodying the essence of the spiritual teachings, are we really practicing? If our practice is haphazard, sporadic, or merely performative, will we ever go beyond it?

We have to make a strong effort, so it's good to find a practice that inspires you. But practice is not a game or entertainment. Practice should challenge us. Our practices should regularly take us out of our comfort zone. They may challenge us physically, emotionally, and mentally, putting into question our beliefs and assumptions, our goals and our views, and ultimately our existence and nonexistence. For that to happen, we have to allow a will to the truth to guide our efforts onward.

Ultimately, the purpose of practice is to go beyond practice, to realize directly one's true being. But it's usually not enough to just say so. A person's interests, desires, needs, conditioning, and karmic bonds have to be exhausted. All that has to be burned up in the sacred fire. So until practice is no longer needed, practice is helpful and necessary.

Whatever practice you take up — meditation, inquiry, prayer, and so on — the ongoing process builds a bridge between the kindling of the sacred fire and the last vestiges of smoke blown away in nirvana. The purpose of practice is to throw wood on the fire, and to provide opportunities to recognize impermanence, emptiness, and awareness itself. The purpose is to burn up the delusions that keep you from recognizing the immediate and ever-present truth.

The Variety of Practice

When people ask what practice they should be doing, there's no single answer. Unless you're practicing in a particular tradition of prescribed practices, the possibilities are vast and somewhat overwhelming. How do we find the practices most suitable to our situation? A teacher can be very helpful, someone who can listen to where you're at, what difficulties you're facing, what insights you're having, and suggest practices or directions that may be fruitful.

Absent a teacher to guide you, it's good to understand the broad array of available practices. Too many people have a narrow view of what spiritual practice is, and therefore limit the possibilities. That's not necessarily bad, but we could overlook potentially beneficial practices or miss the opportunity to look deeper into what we're already doing.

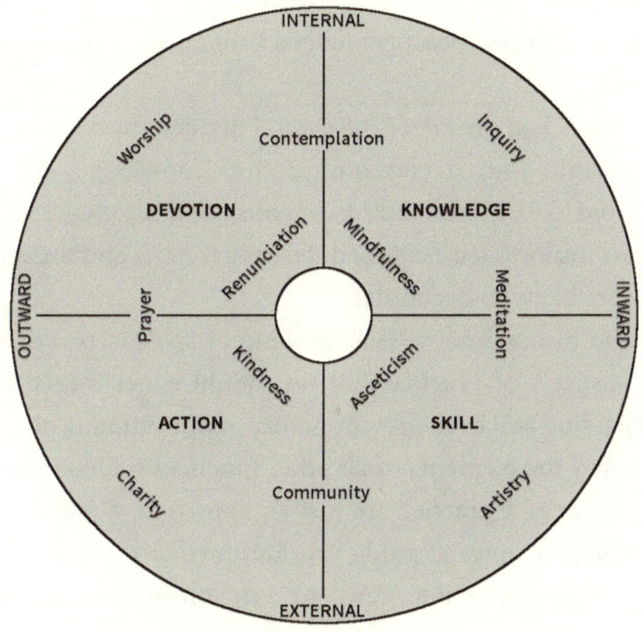

Whatever we do with spiritual intention and mindful attention can be a practice. There's a lot of variety, and if we're searching for the truth in everything, practice can encompass our whole lives. At any given moment, what we want are practices to help dispel the illusions of our conditioning, to show us our attachments and allow us to let go, to liberate thoughts and emotions, and to provide insight through experience.

Because my path was somewhat untraditional, I was exposed to a wide variety of practices: various types of meditation, ritual, prayer, devotion, martial arts, reading, contemplation, reflection, inquiry, lucid dreaming, out-of-body experience, and so on. It was all a part of my path, and although I didn't understand the effects at the time, all these practices helped bring me to the doorstep of awakening.

In *When You are Silent It Speaks*, I divided the broad array of practices into four overarching paths: Knowledge, Devotion, Action, and Skill. In the coming chapters, we'll use these categories to discuss important aspects of different practices and the spiritual traps we're likely to encounter.

In the discussion, we'll be looking at specific practices and various aspects of practice, but we should never forget the all-encompassing and ever-present nature of our ultimate goal. Each practice has the elements of all other practices folded into them. The specifics of a practice are just an approach, a place to start, with some principles to guide you. But meditation, for example, or prayer, compassion, and so on, ultimately encompass everything. Follow any practice to its ultimate end and you will discover the truth itself.

The Elements of Practice

With so many possibilities available for spiritual practice, up to and including the whole circumstance and trajectory of our lives, with all the ups and downs, what can be said about the elements of practice? And how can we make the most of any spiritual practice, whatever it may be?

When practices range so widely — from prayer to charity, meditation to pilgrimage, precepts to transgression, chanting to silence, let alone pursuits as wide ranging as martial arts to painting — it's tempting to think there's no common thread. Especially when we consider the whole of our lives and all the twists and turns, each path seems totally unique.

Common elements emerge only when seen at the proper level of magnification. When we focus on the outer details, prayer and dancing seem to have very little in common. But someone who has reached an exalted level of dancing may tell you otherwise. When we focus inward deeply, all practices appear to have similar core elements, which I have characterized with the four modes: Focusing, Observing, Manipulating, and Emptying. They're just names, but they're good lenses for understanding what these elements are.

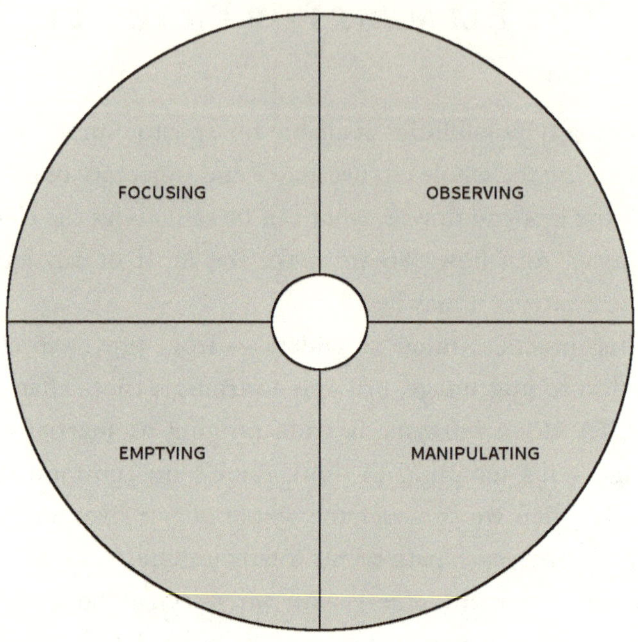

Focusing

Focusing is fundamental to practice, because at the most basic level it's just showing up. If your practice is meditation but you never sit on the cushion, your practice will be inadequate, to say the least. If we don't even show up, we can't expect much — and that's just the beginning of Focusing. We also have to be present, aware, and attentive. We have to train the body and mind to be fully focused on the practice, to be "in the zone," so to speak. If we show up to practice, but the whole time we're just thinking about what we're going to have for dinner or what we said to that person earlier, it's not so good. We have to be able to focus.

Observing

Once we're focused, Observing can come into play. We have to look at what's going on with a critical eye. What we see will naturally change with more practice and deeper understanding. In my martial arts training, my teacher told me to look for tension and fear in others — see where it is, how it arises and accumulates, how it shapes the body, thoughts, actions, et cetera. At the beginning, seeing tension didn't make sense and I couldn't see it, but eventually it was plain as day. We have to try to see the unseen. It *seems* impossible, but it starts with Observing, just really seeing what we *do* see. Whatever our practice, we need to pay attention and observe what is happening, in ourselves, in our surroundings, and in others.

Manipulating

Observing ends and Manipulating begins as soon as we try to change or affect what's happening. Many practices have an overarching aspect of manipulation, since we're often practicing with intention to affect an outcome. Manipulating involves acquiring skills, working with internal states, controlling the body and mind, transforming negative emotions, inducing visions and out-of-body experiences, et cetera. In the martial arts example above, once we're able to observe tension and fear in others, we can develop skill in manipulating it — to control, destroy, or heal. In meditation, we clarify the mind. In prayer, we purify our longing for God alone. In good deeds, we cultivate love and compassion. All willful doing beyond pure observation is manipulation.

Emptying

Finally, we come to Emptying. Of course, it's the hardest one to talk about. I can only point toward it here, and give you a vague idea. It's best described in the negative, in that it's not any of the other three modes, although all are contained within it. Emptying is letting go. We let go of Focusing by letting go of the focuser. We let go of Observing by letting go of the observer. And we let go of Manipulating by letting go of the manipulator. So really, it's letting go of the doer. One is fully present, but *you* are nowhere. Everything happens of its own accord. Within our practice, in moments of self abandon, in profound devotion, in truly selfless deeds, and when we venture beyond the mind, we may glimpse its fullness. But even the novice must empty their cup continuously, for the very purpose of practice is to empty ourselves of views, concepts, and conditioning.

The Process of Practice

Practice doesn't exist to improve, entertain, or please our egos. Instead, practice aims to transcend the ego. The fire is meant to burn up this individual, self-centered, bundle of thoughts we take ourselves to be. So while we can bring ourselves to the fire by engaging in earnest practice and setting our intention to let go, the fire itself does the work.

In the same way a knife cannot cut itself, the ego cannot transcend itself. Any action by the ego only reinforces the egoic view. That's why various practices exist to aid us in letting go. The process of practice is one of progressive clarification of ego and mind-body identification. Clarification could also be called "purification" or "deconstruction." We could give an even more general name, like "the work" or "the process," but the essence is always the same. That essence is letting go of and transcending the ego-self and all particular views. Although we may not realize it until the very end, from the very beginning the way is *selflessness.*

While awakening itself is sudden and spontaneous, practice can be seen as progressive and unfolding. The unfolding involves fractal-like recursions on multiple fronts, but we can consider the process as generally progressive. In any case, our experience of practice is likely to *appear* as unfolding over time.

Progress in practice passes through discernible stages on the spiritual path. While the details of these stages may vary according to the person and the specifics of a practice or tradition, we can characterize the stages as follows:

1. **Contact:** Exposure to and interest in life, teachings, and practice.
2. **Enthusiasm:** Excitement over new thoughts, practices, insights, and experiences.
3. **Commitment:** Initiation and consistent engagement with practice.
4. **Clarification:** Working to see through, purify, and let go of fears, confusion, misunderstandings, disturbing thoughts, negative emotions, paradoxical teachings, enigmatic insights, troubling experiences, and spiritual traps.
5. **Disillusionment:** Dissatisfaction with all views.
6. **Direct Inquiry:** Direct investigation into the nature of self and experience.
7. **Self-emptying:** Cessation of seeking, profound surrender of self and world, and the falling away of all views, doubts, and beliefs.
8. **Enlightenment:** Recognition, direct knowledge, and realization of the One.

Note that only stages 2-6 really pertain to practice, and Enlightenment itself isn't actually a stage. Realization is all encompassing, beyond stages, levels, and locations altogether. I've

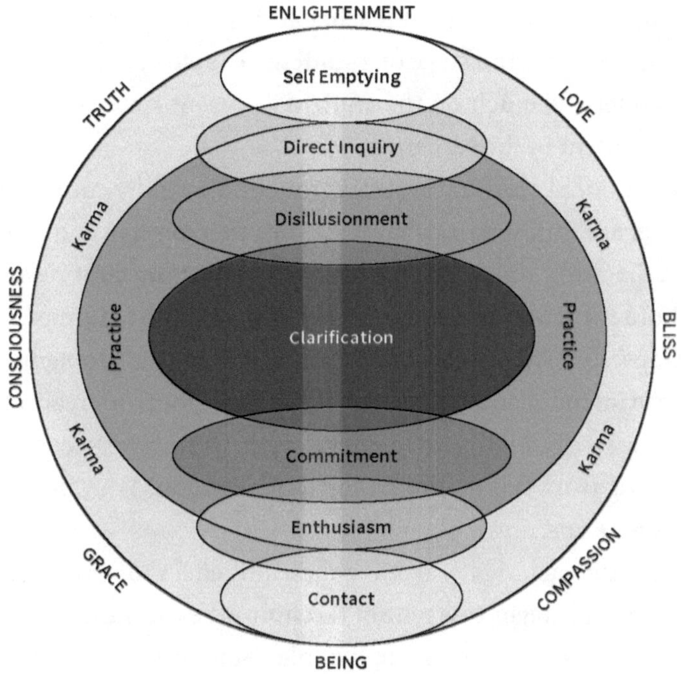

included it only to present a complete progression. Practitioners pass through these stages with varying timeframes and levels of intensity, according to their individual makeup, earnestness, and effort. They can regress, change practices and start over, or change practices and continue where they left off. They may skip ahead, skip around, or be in multiple stages at once. This is all possible, but these are the general stages and order of progression.

Throughout the stages of practice, we can engage in all four paths (Knowledge, Devotion, Action, and Skill) and all four modes (Focusing, Observing, Manipulating, and Emptying). While we may be exposed to a wide range of teachings, the teachings are often stage specific. A good teacher will naturally respond to the disposition, state, and stage of a student. The effect of any teaching is dependent as much on the student's present state and stage as on the content of the teaching.

Traditional teaching systems sometimes rigidly control what students are exposed to, what teachings they receive and in what order. Looking ahead is not allowed, not from any desire to withhold the truth, but rather to avoid misunderstandings, spiritual traps, stymied progress, and even psychological problems. The rules are intended to best insure the potential for truth realization. Even those practicing in a more open framework can learn something from this method. Stop daydreaming! Your practice is always here and now.

Certain teachings only have their full effect for practitioners in a particular stage. This type of teaching is best done directly. For the practitioner, traps are inevitable, but ultimately, the right teachings find their way to those who are ready to hear them. Those who are not ready yet will simply not get the full effect. That's okay — there's some benefit at any stage, and planted seeds come to fruition in time.

Whether teachings are delivered in a strict progression or given freely to all, this process and these stages are at play in the practitioner. Understand there may be some teachings and practices that don't make sense just due to our current stage. That's why it's so important to trust the process and practice with earnestness, even if we don't fully understand. The only way to actually see where the path leads is to throw ourselves into practice and go through the process until we reach the end.

The Hologram Metaphor

I'd like to briefly talk about holograms. A hologram metaphor illustrates that even a single instance of a simple practice contains the entire teaching. Within practice lies the whole of the four paths, the whole of the four modes, and the whole of what lies *beyond* beyond.

A hologram is a three-dimensional image created by a two-dimensional recording of an interference pattern. The technical details aren't important here. As a metaphor, what's important is a peculiar behavior of holographic images. Every subsection of a holographic image contains all the information to create the whole image.

Cutting an ordinary photographic image in half results in two halves, each containing only one half of the original image. If you cut those in half, you get four, one-quarter images, and so on. Cutting a holographic image in half, on the other hand, results in two full images. If you cut those in half you will have four full images, and so on. The images may be smaller instances, but each contains the complete information that was in the original larger image.

While our practice may unfold over a lifetime, just a single instance of meditating, a single utterance of a mantra, or a single encounter with an awakened teacher contains the entirety of that practice's transformational potential. It may take a lifetime and many repetitions to unravel it, to reveal the One Image, but it's all there from the very beginning.

That's why, for example, Dogen Zenji taught that simply practicing meditation *is* enlightenment itself.

Each time you engage in a sincere practice, you are engaging in the entirety of your life, the entirety of the universe, and the entirety of absolute being, beyond being and nonbeing. A single moment of earnest practice is a monumental undertaking far beyond any human comprehension.

What this means for our experience of practice is that we can return, again and again, to the same practice and perceive greater and greater depth. Each time we look with fresh eyes, we see something new, or see something in a new way. For within the practice is a holographic-like representation of everything.

Engaging in Practice

Before really delving into our discussion of practice, let's reiterate some principles covered in the Practices section of *That Which is Before You*. These ideas can be considered as guidelines for engaging in spiritual practice: intention, contrast, consistency, inquiry, and responsibility. Whatever your direction or approach, they're likely to play a role in your ongoing practice, so they're worth reviewing, and we'll add an important addition, as well.

Intention

Consider your intention for undertaking any practice to begin with. Are you truly intent on finding a way to let go of yourself? Do you really want to discover the truth, no matter what it is? Or are you just trying to acquire something for yourself — some mastery, some credential, or some sort of experience?

Your true intention matters, and you are well advised to set your intention and recall it regularly. For there is a sense in which practices function at a super-conscious level. With intention, practices clear a path for allowing the cycle of self-identification to break, and give permission for you to let go.

Contrast

Noticing contrast is an important aspect of evaluating practice. All things become intelligible through contrast, and practice is no different. Paying attention to contrast provides opportunities to recognize change and impermanence, to evaluate relative progress, and to transcend duality.

Cultivate sensitivity and awareness within your practice and in everyday activities. Note how practice affects your body-mind, others, and the world. Look for contrast between things and nothing, between the ever changing and the ever present, between diversity and all-encompassing oneness.

Consistency

The consistency of your practice is one of the most important factors in determining its impact. Consistency is magic! Doing something once in a while is totally different from making it a regular or daily practice. Without some real consistency, it will be difficult to notice significant contrast. Occasional effort may yield some small results, but real transformative change only happens with consistency.

Inquiry

Whatever your approach, when seeking the truth, some measure of inquiry is essential. Feel free to ask your teacher questions, of course, but more importantly, ask yourself questions and don't be afraid to consider whatever answers arise. Even about simple aspects of practice, it's good to ask questions. *What happens if I do it this way? How much of my practice is carrying over to the rest of my life? What is really distracting me?* And so on. The possible questions are endless, but just being in the habit of asking questions will help you notice contrast and recognize where your practice needs to go next.

Responsibility

Finally, the responsibility for your practice is yours and yours alone. A teacher may point, but you have to look. Instruction may guide, but you have to pay attention and do the work. There is no substitute for your own sincerity, earnestness, and effort. Ultimately, the truth can only be discovered for oneself. Nobody can give it to you. I can't stress this enough. Whatever your practice or path, whoever your teacher is, engaging with sincerity, earnestness, and effort is the surest path to transformation. Nobody can do the work for you. Only you can discover who you really are.

Play

If I could add one point here, it would be to include a sense of play. Of course, there are times to practice very seriously and intensely, but don't take *yourself* too seriously — that would be counter-productive. Make ample room for joy! Make space in which to explore, to try things out, to fail, and to laugh wholeheartedly. A balance between seriousness and play is an important aspect of sincere practice.

PART TWO

THE FOUR DIRECTIONS

Wherein we discuss the four paths of seeking,
major practices, and most common spiritual traps.

2

PATHS TO REALIZATION

As I prepared for adult confirmation in the Catholic church, our candidates group was exposed to a variety of practices. Of course, we attended mass and studied teachings, but that's a given. More importantly, we formed a community of practitioners and worked together toward our spiritual goals. We visited other churches with diverse congregations and practices. We said prayers together and created our own rituals. We went out to the larger community and worked in service for others, especially the poor. We opened ourselves up to inquiry and introspection. Ultimately, we made a vow, renouncing the glamour of evil and professing our faith in God.

I mention this as an example to illustrate how the path, even one episode in one person's journey, can push us into many different areas of practice. In retrospect, that challenging diversity of practice made for an excellent program and a great experience. It forced us to engage with a variety of people, places, and practices, and to put ourselves into situations that pushed the boundaries of our conditioned comfort zone — all for the sake of our search for God, Truth, and Salvation.

There are an infinite number of discrete practices, many aspects of the path, and many approaches to the Truth. To better understand this variety, we can look at the four primary pathways: Knowledge, Devotion, Action, and Skill. The categories appear in a variety of traditions and cultures under different names. Regardless of background, they should hold some relevance for everyone.

The four paths can be mapped onto a mandala with one axis representing focus (internal or external) and the other representing direction (inward or outward). Each type of practice can be placed on the mandala, according to whether the focus is internal or external and whether the direction of the practice leads inward or outward.

For example: Self-Inquiry has an internal focus and its direction is inward. Worship also has an internal focus but its direction is outward. Charity has an external focus and its direction is outward. Martial arts has an external focus, but as a spiritual practice, its direction is inward.

The categories are mind-created. They're not mutually exclusive or immutable. In reality, inside and outside are one. So discreet practices contain elements of all four pathways, and each practitioner's journey could wander all over the map. We can use the map to characterize different types of practice, but all practices are related and the full spectrum is available.

According to each person's inclinations and experience, different paths will appeal to them as potentially fruitful. Why does one person gravitate toward meditation and another toward

worship? Why does one put forth effort toward charity while another puts their effort toward self mastery?

One path is not inherently more right than another. Although we all face similar obstacles and the truth is truth for all, each person's heart is a unique puzzle. We work out the mystery by sincerely engaging with the spiritual journey, and by putting forth effort in whatever practices appear in the context of our lives.

Put all options on the table. We should not hesitate to explore the practices we're inclined toward. Nor should we discount those that don't appeal to us. Sometimes the practices we *don't* want to do are the most helpful and illuminating. We should not hesitate to focus with intensity on a single practice, nor should we reject exploring many practices.

Please understand, even before we get into it, all the paths are really the same path. The four paths — Knowledge, Devotion, Action, and Skill — are just a way to talk about generalities in practice and seeking. To that end, they can be helpful, but don't ignore a particular practice because you think you're on a different path. That's nonsense. We're all on the same path! And we can learn from everything.

Wherever our journey leads us, be it seemingly down a path of Knowledge, Devotion, Action, or Skill, in reality there is only *the* path, which contains various elements according to the individual. If this path is followed all the way to the end, by whatever circuitous route, the same Truth is revealed. So whatever traditions, teachers, and practices present themselves in the context of our lives, we should just set our resolve on the sincerity of our search. We should cultivate an earnestness that will help us put effort into practice and follow where the path leads.

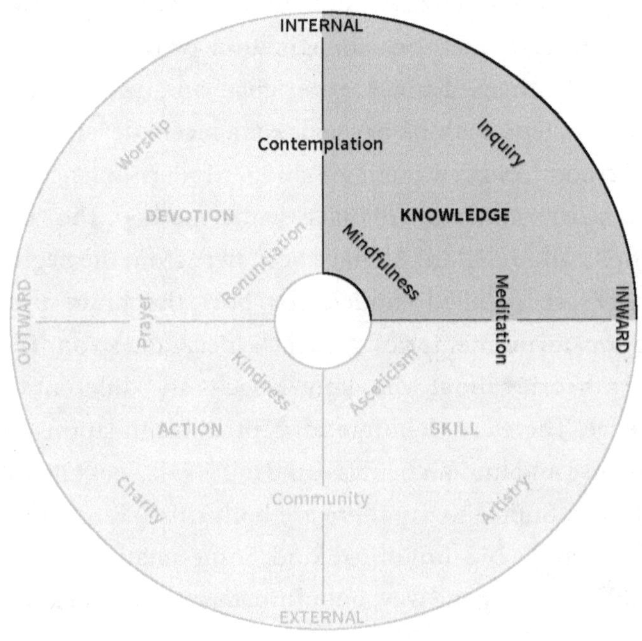

3

PATH OF KNOWLEDGE

Throughout time and across cultures, human beings have tried to understand and articulate what life is. *Why am I here? What is existence? Who am I? What is the world? What am I meant to do? How can I live the best life? Where did I come from? What will happen after I die?* And so on. These types of questions give rise to the path of Knowledge.

Imagination and reason are the mind's essential tools for addressing these questions. Imagination provides possibilities. Reason tests them against experience and prior predicates. Although we tend to think of science as a recent development, the basic method has been there all along. Modern science is just a refinement or codification of that essential method. The same with philosophy and religion. All have been here from the beginning.

There are detailed models for how the brain processes perception, forms memories, generates ideas, and so on. There are complex theories about what knowledge is and different types of knowledge. There are elaborate conceptual formulations for how the universe and human beings came to be. We won't go into any of that here. Suffice to say there are both small, limited kinds of knowledge and a big, unlimited kind. Some small knowledge can certainly help along the way, but ultimately it's the big knowledge we're interested in.

For those who venture on the path of Knowledge, it's not enough to know the names of things and model their workings. It's not enough to know the procedures, maps, and intricacies of conceptual formulations. It's not enough to just trust a given explanation. We're looking for *real* answers. We're looking for a truth that cannot be disputed, disproved, or undermined. We're looking for a truth that completely satisfies. We're looking for a truth that ends suffering. We're looking for a truth that unveils profound peace.

This path appeals to seekers with a strong intellect, a logical mind, and an inclination toward figuring things out for themselves. Often such people have philosophic and scientific outlooks.

The focus of their path is internal and mind centered. Their direction is inward, turning the mind on itself and directing the faculties of the intellect toward understanding direct experience. The purest form of practice is self-inquiry.

The challenge seekers face is going beyond the mind. Because we're so strongly identified with the mind and its activities, we tend to search for our answers there. Even when extensive mind activity fails to yield the results we seek, we're at a loss as to where else to look. We question everything except the thinker, but ultimately we must question that, too. We must go beyond the mind to find the knowledge we seek.

The Importance of Inward Curiosity

The most important quality to cultivate on the path of Knowledge is curiosity. A strong will to the truth works in concert with curiosity to fuel the fire of inquiry. In the quest for knowledge, we should be willing to look where others might not and follow wherever the journey leads. We have to overcome our fear of failure and of various potential answers or outcomes, in order to look and see what's really there.

If we're fixed in our ideas and beliefs, satisfied and complacent about our ego and worldview, we will lack the curiosity necessary to push forward on the path of Knowledge. But if we start from a place of wonder and humility, accepting that we really don't know the answers we seek, then we'll have a good mindset for this quest.

The search for knowledge entails looking inward. Curiosity about what we think of as "the external world," must be put into the perspective of the observer of this world. The scientific-minded person, whose primary curiosity is aimed outward, must eventually turn the mind on itself, questioning the role and nature of the mind and consciousness.

Recently, there's been a strong drive to understand consciousness, thoughts, emotions, and so on in terms of neuroscience, and certainly the correlations are interesting and useful. However, being curious about brains and neuroscience is still essentially *outward* curiosity. Brains are things in the world and studying them is studying the external world. *Inward* curiosity means studying experience through experience, and turning the mind on itself.

It's not enough to be curious about the external world without being curious about yourself. After all, who is the observer of this world? Without this observer, there would be no world. All external objects, all worlds, brains, and minds, come and go within consciousness itself. Awareness is the root and origin of all experience.

There's no point in belaboring this too much, as we have already discussed it extensively in previous books. But it's the antidote to our externally focused worldviews and strong mind-body identification. Although ultimately there is no inside or outside, at some point, *inward* curiosity becomes key to the path of Knowledge.

Reading Books and Sacred Texts

The wisdom of those who went before us is written in innumerable books and sacred scriptures. For many, encountering such texts is an important step on the path of Knowledge. For some, reading and studying may be a significant part of their practice. Since you're reading this now, we know books have some role in your journey.

Every twist and turn of my journey was accompanied by books that pointed out the way and pushed me forward. Books like *Guide to Yoga Meditation* by Richard Hittleman, *Freedom from the Known* by J. Krishnamurti, and *Zen Beyond All Words* by Wolfgang Kopp were all instrumental on my spiritual journey. Even after awakening, books like *The Way of Selflessness* by Joel Morwood, *Talks* by Ramana Maharshi, and *I Am That* by Sri Nisargadatta Maharaj helped me better understand and articulate what had happened. And these are just a few examples.

The great gift of such books cannot be overestimated! They are instrumental in the unfolding of human consciousness. We are blessed to come across such gems as aids on our path toward knowledge. How we process such texts depends on what stage we're at on our journey. We're not assured of recognizing the full value of the teachings, and what we get out of our reading is very much tied to what we're ready to hear and if the time is right. So how should we approach reading?

On the one hand, we are where we are, and our mind is as it is at the moment of any encounter, so we will respond accordingly.

On the other hand, the encounter itself plays a role in unraveling the mind, so some kind of intention is helpful.

If what you read is baffling — and let's be honest, a lot of spiritual literature can be — don't worry. Just keep an open mind. Absorb the material without grasping or aversion. If possible, try to sort out *what* is being said, but refrain from making judgments. If you can't even understand what is being said, that's okay too. It does not follow that your reading is pointless. The effect of such texts can start far below the level of conscious understanding. So read on, even if you must approach the text as a kind of enigmatic poetry.

If a book makes sense, if it rings true or is in accord with your experience, then consider putting the teachings into practice. Don't just grasp at what's being said intellectually. Try to look where the text is pointing. Try to do what the text is instructing you to do. Attempt to see for yourself what's indicated. The more effort we put forth in our response, the greater the opportunity for insight and transformation.

Finally, remember that rereading can yield novel results! Those who reread books notice new aspects of the content and often have a deeper understanding on the second or third reading. Just because you've read a book, don't assume you've understood everything it has to offer or benefited from its full potential. Each time we return to a text, we are a different person and at a different place on our journey.

Insight Meditation

Taking up meditation practice will generally involve calming the body and mind. For some people, this is the only goal. Calming the body-mind is good, of course, and has many benefits for our health and well-being. On the path of Knowledge, however, calming meditation should be seen as only a preparatory step, a prerequisite for exploring deeper states of absorption and engaging in insight meditation.

There are many types of meditation and specific instructions for practice. Having never been an exclusive follower of one school of meditation practice, my interest lies more in recognizing the unifying elements of various approaches. As already mentioned, I have identified these elements as Focusing, Observing, Manipulating, and Emptying.

Calming the body-mind enough to sit quietly for a while just covers the first layer of Focusing. It's necessary before we can really start to practice Observing, Manipulating, and Emptying. Once a minimum level of concentration is achieved, we can start to look at what's happening without getting too caught up by it. For example:

- What sensations and thoughts appear?
- How do they arise and subside?
- Where do they come from?
- Where do they go?

- What happens when you look at them?
- What happens when you grasp on to them?
- What happens when you try to push them away?
- Is it possible to just drop them?
- What happens when you drop everything?

All this must be understood, not through thoughts and words, but through experience. Within dedicated practice, there are multiple layers to Focusing, Observing, Manipulating, and Emptying. A base level of Focusing allows for a base level of Observing, Manipulating, and Emptying. From Emptying we can enter into basic samadhis. When we return to Focusing, we find a deeper level, and so on. Progress, as long as we're allowing for it, can be seen as a kind of spiral, returning to the various elements with new understanding.

Focusing is developed by maintaining attention on a singular object, such as the breath, a stone, or a candle flame. Even in the case of open awareness, focus is developed by maintaining attention on awareness itself. When Observing, we watch the contents and processes that arise within consciousness, noting how all sensations, emotions, thoughts, memories, et cetera, arise, change, and subside. When Manipulating, we play with affecting the contents — shaping perceptions and processes, dropping thoughts, transforming negativity, withdrawing from sensation, and so on.

Deep states of meditation are possible, and extraordinary experiences can happen. They may serve to open the mind and push us ahead on our journey. Without insight, however, they can just as easily become a trap, or lead us further into our delusions. A good teacher is invaluable! Through practice, we're not seeking special states or experiences so much as insight into impermanence, dissatisfaction, and the nature of self.

See how the contents of consciousness come and go. Nothing can withstand the continuous light of awareness. That's impermanence! See how all objects within consciousness — even the most wonderful thoughts or pleasant sensations — eventually leave you wanting. Nothing can truly satisfy you. That's dissatisfaction! See how the locus of identity cannot be found in any particular thing. Nothing can be found which constitutes the self. That's the nature of self! It's beyond all things.

Direct Inquiry

At the heart of the path of Knowledge is direct inquiry into the nature of self, perception, and the world. To approach questions such as *Who am I? What is the nature of time and space? What is the nature of the universe and reality?* and *How do I exist?* involves an inquiry that goes to the very edge of the mind and beyond.

All direct inquiry could ultimately be termed self-inquiry. Even when the inquiry relates to the world — to time or space for example — the directness makes it personal. An inquiry into what initially seems to be external progresses inward to involve both perception and self. The question of *who* or *what* is aware, naturally comes into play. Since such an inquiry could actually begin anywhere, I broadly refer to it as direct inquiry.

Traditionally, we might encounter teachings stating that seer, seeing, and seen are all one. That's interesting to ponder, of course, but the teaching is only pointing the way. We have to verify. We have to do our own direct inquiry if we're ever going to find out for ourselves. This kind of knowledge cannot rely on others. Nor can it rely on words, thoughts, ideas, or concepts. It's *direct* knowledge.

When speaking of general inquiry, we're usually looking for articulated answers. We ask a verbal-conceptual question and we are seeking a verbal-conceptual answer, be it a statement of observed fact, opinion, or logical conclusion. Most people approach all questions like that, and it works well for practical matters. When it comes to the most fundamental questions, however, this approach is wholly inadequate.

Direct inquiry may begin with what seems like a verbal-conceptual question, but when we begin to search for the answer, sooner or later it becomes clear that no verbal-conceptual answer will satisfy us. If we ask "Who am I?" or "What is space?" a multitude of verbal responses may come to mind, but if we're serious about discovering the answer, we must admit that such answers, however mundane or sophisticated, are not truly satisfying.

Such questions are pointing beyond any verbal-conceptual answer. Although some verbal-conceptual thoughts may get the work started, eventually we'll come to a logical dead end. We come to the end of our particular line of thinking, and still we have not reached a conclusion. Usually, because we're fixated on finding an answer in a thought, we turn around, retrace our steps, and take up a different line of thinking.

Just when we think our inquiry is sputtering out is actually the beginning of direct inquiry. Instead of retracing our steps or taking up yet another line of thinking, what if we lingered there at the edge of the mind, in that uncomfortable silence that booms beyond the limits of our thoughts? What if we took a few steps out into the non-answer we have come to? What if, having knocked, we just remained there, waiting for the door to be answered.

In direct inquiry, we must ultimately endeavor to seek the answer in direct experience, beyond views. If we inquire into time, for example, we must actually *see* time. If we inquire into space, we must actually *touch* space. If we inquire into the self, we must actually *recognize* consciousness itself. Direct inquiry always leads beyond, until at last we come to true knowledge.

The Trap of Conceptualism

Traps abound on every path. They're all essentially the same kind of obstacles, but each path offers its own particular flavors. On the path of Knowledge, conceptualizing is pretty much inevitable as we struggle to reach an understanding we can understand. But as our practice progresses, conceptualism becomes an obstacle to reaching an understanding which is beyond understanding.

Conceptualism is reliance on some kind of intellectual understanding with the belief this constitutes real knowledge or wisdom. As we receive teachings and endeavor to practice, attempts to understand through the intellect can be helpful up to a point. It's a natural starting place for this path. If, however, we fixate on intellectual constructs or come to believe this conceptual understanding is the goal, we have been ensnared in a trap.

These traps can be subtle. The fact of the matter is we're already ensnared, through conditioning, in many conceptual views which we take to be reality. Concepts are the glue which holds minds and worlds together, so new concepts can be very seductive. We may integrate them into existing concepts, or trade one conceptual view for another, without ever realizing we're already trapped.

How can we avoid this when, as I said, it's inevitable?

First, just be aware this is the case. We're *already* embroiled in layer upon layer of conceptual views and conceptual experience. Conceptualism is the predominant experience of our day-to-day lives. Naturally, when we encounter a teacher or hear about awakening, we treat enlightenment as another view to grasp, another experience to have, another thing to know. We go about trying to learn everything we can about it, but ultimately, enlightenment is not a *thing.*

Ordinary knowledge is knowledge of things, of object-events and concepts, which are amalgams of object-events, other concepts, and their relationships to each other. This path we're on leads to a different kind of knowledge. It's not knowledge of any particular thing. It's knowledge of the source of all things. It's knowledge of foundational truth. It's knowledge of *nothing* and *everything.* It's knowledge, through recognition, of consciousness itself, without subjects, objects, or events. It's knowledge of reality itself and all-encompassing bliss. It's pure knowing, devoid of concepts or content.

So on the path of Knowledge, keep pushing the boundaries of various conceptual views you have, acquire, and are tempted by. When you read books, receive teachings, practice meditation and inquiry, try not to latch onto any particular view, the way you might a new conceptual worldview. Instead, burn up your views in the sacred fire. Allow teachings and practices to take effect on their own accord, without grasping or resistance. Remember the instructions, teachings, and practices are only a means of pointing toward a knowledge that transcends all things — all thoughts, all concepts, and all views.

Putting Knowledge into Practice

The purpose of the overall discussion here is three-fold: to illuminate the variety of approaches to practice, ward off obstacles, and inspire seekers in their efforts. To this last point, how can the path of Knowledge be put into practice by anyone? After all, actually attempting to do the practices and putting effort into them is what matters.

Self-inquiry based on direct observation and experience is at the heart of the path. Our aim is direct inquiry into fundamental questions such as *Who am I? What am I? What is this experience?* Through investigation, we discover all conceptual answers are fundamentally flawed, inadequate, or unsatisfying. What's revealed as false naturally falls away. Then we can see the reality beyond, wherein lies our true answer.

The main difficulty is our conditioned conceptual approach to all questions. We're always looking for a conceptual view or explanation of how things are. So when we start down a path of self-inquiry, we habitually look for, gravitate toward, and cling to various conceptual views, rather than attempt to observe and experience the one who is seeking.

A natural place to consolidate our efforts is with regular meditation practice. Meditation helps develop the kind of focused, patient, calm mind conducive to inquiry. Meditation provides practice in directly observing and manipulating the mind. And meditation works to break the conditioned instinct to cling to conceptual views. Finally, meditation provides opportunities for insight into what lies beyond the mind.

Find a time in your regular routine to sit quietly for ten to twenty minutes, with no distractions or activities. Commit to doing this regularly and consistently. Learn some fundamental meditation practices, such as focusing on a meditation object or the breath, watching thoughts, dropping thoughts, looking at the space between thoughts, and open awareness. Explore these practices in your sitting to develop Focusing, Observing, Manipulating, and Emptying.

Persevere in regular practice, no matter how difficult or boring, and over time note changes in your experience and attitudes. Remember the stages of practice. Expect struggles. Expect disillusionment. Keep going! And when you inquire into the nature of self, look not for an answer, but for that one who is asking the question. Real insight never comes from clinging to concepts or chasing after new ideas, but always through letting go of present thoughts.

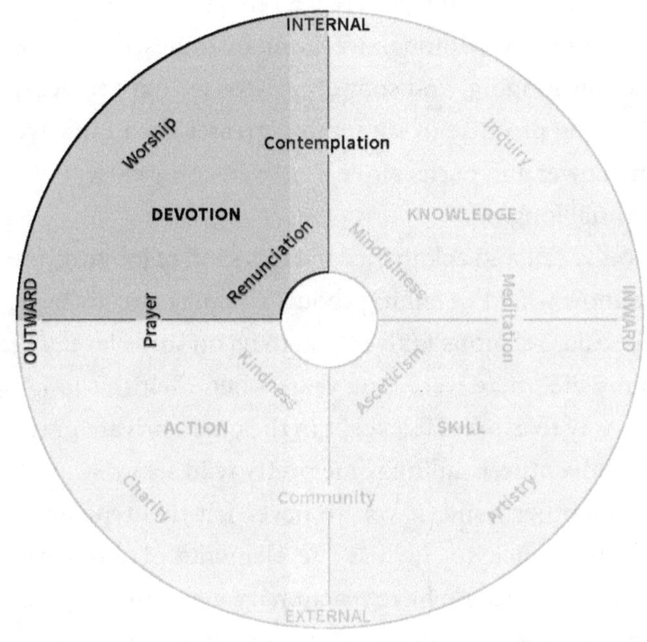

4

PATH OF DEVOTION

God has a billion names and a billion faces, appearing to the mind as innumerable forms across time and space. With an ache in their hearts, one way or another, people have always sought peace in God. Through stories and songs, rituals and prayers, penance and pilgrimage, we acknowledge the divine, struggle to be faithful, and cultivate love on the path of Devotion.

Many who tread this path feel an inexplicable longing which nothing can satisfy. Although we try many things, nothing worldly can ease this longing, and sooner or later we have to accept that fact. Only the promise of something greater than ourselves, of a supreme power and perfect love, can even come close to touching this spiritual longing.

If you've felt and acknowledged this kind of longing, then you already know what I'm talking about. You may already be devoted to a particular religious faith or you may, on some level, wish you did. In my life, there were long years when I felt this longing but had no a way to express it, except in the quiet, private prayers of a doubtful adventurer sailing some pretty wild seas.

On the other hand, if you've never felt this type of longing, don't be too quick to dismiss the elements of this path or its potential. Many people have reactionary views to religious devotion. The reasons are multitudinous, including negative personal experience, institutional crimes, theological infantilism, and global, historical shifts in philosophical worldviews. Whatever the reasons, longing for truth, love, and liberation has not vanished. Such spiritual longing may take different forms, but if you look, you will find it.

Those on the path of Devotion are drawn to a higher power, which takes shape in the mind as images, concepts, persons, or stories. To follow the path of Devotion is to acknowledge this higher power, even without fully understanding it, and to entrust one's life and activities to that. When followed, love may blossom … and eventually, profound surrender.

This path appeals to people who have already had some kind of spiritual experience or intuitive connection to a higher power, but are still seeking fulfillment. While the focus of their path is internal, the direction is outward, toward an image or concept of the divine. Practice could be through organized religion, but could just as easily be a private and personal devotion.

A common mistake on this path lies in taking the trappings of faith — the images and stories, and the particulars of practice — for the truth itself. Ultimately, the real challenge is to go beyond our own divine image or concept. The reality of God transcends everything, even divine images and concepts. So in surrendering ourselves to God, we must surrender even those ideas which we hold so dear.

The Importance of Faith

Faith goes hand in hand with the path of Devotion, and plays an important role from beginning to end. Faith doesn't necessarily involve a detailed accounting of beliefs, as in some religions. But devotion involves acknowledging a higher power, and some faith in a higher power is essential, even if only a tiny seed.

Faith is not blind profession of belief. Anybody can do that — it's just words. Although professing belief can be a part of the journey, the role of faith and our journey in faith is much larger than that. Faith is the struggle to *really* believe and ultimately to *know,* beyond words and with eyes wide open.

Like prayer itself, the journey of faith progresses from just acknowledging a higher power to trusting that higher power, and finally, to loving and surrendering to that higher power. As devotion increases, the self decreases. Profound surrender is not far off. Ultimately, we give up the individual self entirely to live in Truth itself.

Those who think they have things pretty-well figured out may delude themselves into thinking they have faith. But actually they are lacking it. Unwilling to genuinely grapple with uncertainty and doubts, they bury their heads in the sands of blind belief, forestalling their journey rather than engaging with it.

Faith requires a willingness to struggle toward perfection, even without knowing how. Because of this, faith requires ever-greater reliance on the higher power itself, even with limited knowledge. To shield oneself from this struggle is a trap. That's why faith is so important on this path.

We must trust this is all going somewhere, that the process of our practice and the situations of our lives are leading us — sometimes gently, sometimes harshly — toward a love and perfection that is beyond our comprehension.

Following a Religion

When we enter into a religion, much attention is given to how to follow that particular faith. What to read, how to dress, when to pray, how to act, and many similar details are considered. The details are endless and enticing. It's easy to obsess over details, and to a certain extent, there's nothing wrong with a few details to get started. But much less attention is given to the broad trajectory of our spiritual journey.

It's actually quite rare to see general advice on how to follow a religion. In other words, regardless of which religion we enter into and whether entered by inheritance or choice, how should we go about it? Let's consider what that generalized advice might be.

Practicing a religion is almost always characterized by the particulars. But if you're seeking deeper insight, keep in mind the particulars are like an image in a stained-glass window. Illumined from beyond, colors and forms appear, stories are depicted and concepts illustrated for all to see. And yet, these particulars are only the trappings of a deeper mystery. The truth is the pure light beyond the window of our religion. Without that light, no image appears. It alone is the reality behind all images. The image is only a place for the mind to enter.

Whatever religion we follow, of course we should follow the particulars. To point the way, some kind of window is better than a head full of sand. Listen to and contemplate the teachings. Do the rituals and practices. Recite the prayers. But keep in mind, these things are pointing to a reality beyond the mind's ability to comprehend. So as you cultivate your faith, cultivate a faith in that which is *beyond* your understanding.

Each religion has its conception of the ultimate truth — a story it tells about divinity, reality, and life. They vary from children's stories to mind-boggling philosophies and theologies. Religions are generally adept at serving up whatever level of explanation one prefers or can handle. Just remember that from the most simple to the most complex, from the most concrete to the most abstract, all these conceptions are still only images and ideas.

Nevertheless, as we practice our chosen religion, the general trend of progress moves from the concrete to the abstract. The image in the stained glass window becomes a little more transparent — the glass a bit thinner, the shapes more amorphous, the depictions more abstract, the colors more translucent. But it's still a window. The window lets in the light, but inevitably distorts what passes through and reflects the individual who looks at it. Somehow, within our practice, we must trust more in the light than in the images. We must love this light more than anything — and certainly more than any particular window. After all … life, eons, planets, and suns all pass in a flash. But Truth is eternal.

Devotion to God

To have a devotional practice, we need an object of devotion, a direction to focus our love and efforts. The natural recipient of such attention is our image of the divine or our concept of God. Of course, such images vary greatly and change over time for each practitioner. But without some concept of a higher power, where would we direct our acknowledgement, our trust, our love, and our surrender?

Practitioners who follow a religion likely have a rich body of teachings from which to derive a divine image and a relationship with it. Even secular practitioners likely have a conception of the divine on some level. Who receives and responds to prayers? What power created this universe and the beings in it? Why does anything exist? What is the eternal, supreme reality? A brief but honest survey of your mind's answers will likely reveal something about your concept of the divine.

Believers, of course, will say it's not just a concept. Fair enough. Do the names of and stories about God refer to a reality beyond concepts? I will not dispute it, but when expressed in form and language, those are concept which only *point toward* the divine. Such expressions aren't divine on their own. The supreme power is surely beyond conceptual understanding.

For non-believers, if you search your mind for notions of what reality is or the highest principle, you may find you already have a kind of divine concept. Maybe it's not what you thought God was supposed to be, but nevertheless you have some notion of a higher power — be it the universe, space, physical or metaphysical laws, or reality itself.

Whatever our disposition, a devotion to God cannot be merely devotion to a name or an idea. Nor can we presume to intimately know the reality of God from the beginning of our practice. While we may need an image to focus our efforts, we must keep in mind that any image only points to the reality. So when, in devotion, we pray, chant, sing, worship, and serve others, our actions and our efforts don't just reference a thought or idea, but rather evoke the divine reality and draws us toward that.

Ultimately, devotional practice is a struggle to transcend what is mere image and concept, in order to love what is truly divine.

Devotion to Guru

Sometimes a person or a being appears that brings the truth to our attention and points the way toward realization. How wonderful! They show us — through teachings, experiences, and by example — the liberation, peace, and happiness we seek. And we may respond, if the time is right for us, with acknowledgement, trust, and love.

Devotion to a guru is not so common in the West, due to various cultural attitudes, but it's not something dubious or unseemly. It's not falling under the spell of a harmful cult, which is an important but entirely different topic we will discuss elsewhere. Devotion to a guru is true love for that one who has brought the truth to our attention and pointed the way toward peace.

Honestly, this kind of devotion may sound strange or implausible unless we've experienced it. That's okay — many experiences sound implausible until they happen. In fact, when such an experience does happen, it can be surprising or even shocking. But nevertheless, it's perfectly clear. Loving devotion blossoms for that one who went before us, who pointed toward the truth, and showed us the way.

In my case, I had become a stubborn and somewhat hard-hearted and skeptical person, so while I had some teachers I acknowledged as skilled and trusted for guidance in practice, I didn't fully understand devotion to guru until after my awakening. And maybe that's always the case. For while the guru may appear as a person, the true guru is none other than the Self — the Great Spirit that created the universe and permeates all beings and all worlds, that Reality which is eternal and which transcends entirely existence and non-existence. So ultimately, it may take realization to fully recognize this guru, but once recognized, love is full and abiding.

For those on the path, we must do the best we can to seek out good teachers. Acknowledge those from whom we can learn. Listen attentively to their instruction. Ask thoughtful questions. And put the teachings into consistent practice. All this takes trust and dedication to the path. If you find a good teacher, learn as much as you can from them by devoting yourself to them and their teaching.

Fortunate are those who cross paths with a fully Self-realized teacher. Although at the time we may not consciously recognize such a teacher, and may not know our good fortune, we have received a great gift. We have looked into eyes unclouded by delusion, and so have come face to face with the true guru.

The Trap of Idolatry

As a guy who was given the middle name *Aaron*, and who went to at least a few Sunday school lessons, I was always interested in the story of the golden calf. I wondered why my parents would name me after someone who led the Israelites in the sin of idolatry. Of course, there are other events involving Aaron, but the golden calf is a dramatic story, and the trap of idolatry is the most significant trap on the path of Devotion.

Like the trap of conceptualism, idolatry involves mistaking something, which is not itself reality, for reality itself. In conceptualism, we mistake a thought or an idea for reality itself, while in idolatry we project outward and mistake an image, an object, or an institution for God or the divine reality. They're essentially the same mistake and the same trap. For example, when conceptualization is focused externally and directed onto objects, the result is idolatry.

In Sunday school, it seemed like a fairly easy sin to avoid. Just don't make a big statue and bow down to worship it as a god. Check — no problem. But like most Sunday-school lessons, the message was overly simplistic, culturally myopic, and woefully incomplete. Although bowing down and worshipping a statue as an actual god, rather than as a representation or avatar of God, could amount to idolatry, this trap is much more subtle than that … and much more difficult to avoid.

Idolatry does not lie in crafting statues, looking at them, bowing toward them, nor even in saying prayers before them.

Idolatry is a subtle trap of the heart and mind. Idolatry does not consist of any particular action or image, but rather in forgetting that God transcends all things and thus is beyond all images, words, symbols, concepts, objects, bodies, minds, and thoughts. As soon as we regard the higher power as limited in any way, we're already courting idols. And as soon as we love any particular thing as the truth itself, we're already in sin.

Christianity struggled with this trap over the centuries, debating the veneration of saints and alternately using icons and banning or destroying them for fear of idolatry. Judaism and Islam settled on forbidding any representations of God. Hinduism accepted divine images as helpful for focusing on the spiritual path. Buddhism seems split, with some sects courting a vast pantheon of deities, and others adopting austerity with regard to images. There's no easy or right solution to the trap of idolatry. The fact is, for those who don't really *know* God, idolatry is inevitable. Because we long for God but know only worldly things, we seek for divinity there. Even the traditions themselves and their holy scriptures can become idols in the hearts and minds of followers.

We'll conclude here with a Zen story that illustrates the subtleties of this trap better than any explanation. I first heard this story in a recorded lecture by Alan Watts. I'm reciting it from memory, so please excuse any variations.

On a cold and snowy winter night, a man took shelter in a ruined monastery. To keep himself warm, he lit a fire, using as fuel some of the many wooden Buddha statues that were there in the ruins. Later, a monk joined him, seeking shelter from the cold, but when he saw remnants of a Buddha statue in the fire, he was aghast.

"What are you doing?" the monk said. "You can't burn a Buddha! It's sacrilege! Put out this fire at once."

The man made no move to put out the flames. Instead, he took a stick and began stirring around in the coals at the base of the fire.

"What are doing?" The monk said, still angry about the burning Buddha.

"I'm looking for the mani jewel," the man said, which is a mythic jewel said to be in the head of a Buddha.

"You fool!" the monk said. "You won't find any mani jewel — it's just a wooden Buddha."

"In that case," the man said, "hand me another Buddha for my fire."

Putting Devotion into Practice

Whether or not you believe in God or consider yourself a religious person, some aspects of devotion can be helpful for all practitioners. If you're not currently practicing a religion or some form of devotion, you can still engage in and benefit from this type of practice. How can we get started?

The most important step is to acknowledge a higher power. How you conceive of this higher power is not as important as the basic acknowledgement that we are not in control, and all things unfold in the context of a higher power. That's all.

Once we have some simple acknowledgement of a higher power, perhaps conceived as an idea of God, the universe itself, physical laws, or transcendent reality, we can begin to embrace devotion. The best way to get started is remembering this higher power through small ritual acknowledgements. For example, through thought, gratitude, and prayer.

Make a habit of starting and finishing your day with a thought and prayer given to this power. Before each meal, take a moment to acknowledge the higher power and to be grateful for the food, for this life, for our experiences, and our teachers. This is already the path of Devotion.

You can incorporate some element of ritual into this practice, but it doesn't have to be overly complicated. A bow, gesture, or a few words can be enough. You don't need to understand everything you're doing or comprehend fully what the higher power is. The important thing is just to do it, to consistently remember and acknowledge the higher power.

In all practice, we just do the practice. We can't, on our own, bring about the results we seek. The practice itself and the higher power does its work on us. We learn as we go how to trust the practice and that higher power.

In times of stress or difficulty in life, try to rely on the higher power for support, perspective, and guidance. Aim toward cultivating the kind of trust that helps you let go of unnecessary attachments and concerns. True love doesn't come from clinging, but rather from continuously letting go.

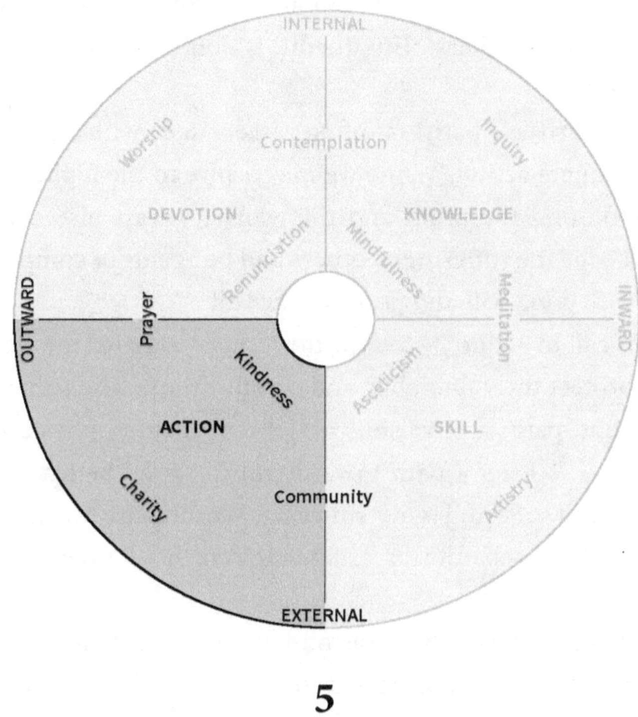

5

PATH OF ACTION

In stories from the great spiritual literature, the troubles of life and the suffering of people take a prominent role. The Buddha, for example, left his life as a prince to seek an end to suffering after witnessing the effects of poverty, disease, and old age. Jesus commanded his followers to heal the sick and cast out demons, to embrace the poor, feed the hungry, and give shelter to those in need. Of course, Buddha and Jesus are not alone in acknowledging the suffering of others. This theme is common to all spiritual literature.

The spiritual path is often associated with a path of compassionate action. While we may aspire to the highest truth, a truth beyond the mind and this world, we are also called to acknowledge the suffering of others and be agents of compassion, acting with good will and peace toward all.

This call to action — to feed the hungry, care for the sick and dying, protect the vulnerable, and comfort those who suffer from fear, doubt, pain, and various afflictions, mental, physical, and spiritual — is itself a path toward truth. For all beings are *one* being, and all suffering is *our* suffering. We all share the same Self, and nobody is separate or excluded from it — even the most wretched evil-doers.

To the extent we can see beyond our ego-self, which sees itself as separate, and see the true Self in others, which is not separate, we thin the veil that separates us from bliss-consciousness. So treating others as oneself, cultivating love and kindness, doing good deeds and behaving with right action are all practices that bring us closer to the truth.

Those already called to this path may not have considered *why* or *how* such actions bring us closer to God, other than God loves all and has pointed us toward the same all-encompassing love. And frankly, that's good enough, if followed. The practice of such action is really what matters, not the rationale. Again, we just do the practice. The process of engagement and the practice itself are what's really transformative.

But for those who stand aloof and don't put forth effort toward loving others, reforming their egos, and doing good deeds, perhaps this rationale will inspire them into action. We can find our true Self by recognizing it in others and acting accordingly. May all beings know the safety, peace, and freedom from doubt the truth alone grants in full. And may the actions of all beings bring this enlightenment to fruition.

The Importance of Compassion

The path of Action begins and ends with compassion. Without compassion, we will not recognize the suffering of others. But with even a taste of genuine compassion, we feel the suffering of others as our own and long to relieve it. A heavy dose can tear open the heart, exposing unexplored regions that can never really be covered up.

Loving kindness, right action, and all good deeds have their roots in compassion. We can follow these practices and the basic feeling of shared suffering from the very beginning to the very end. Ultimately, we may come to experience a compassion that encompasses everything, a compassion that is the very engine of manifest existence.

We hopefully received, as children, some basic lessons about sharing, kindness, and consideration for others. That's good, of course, because it points us in the right direction. But the teaching also has to take root through an experience of shared suffering. That's what opens the heart and really *shows* us the way, if we only dare to follow it.

Too often, as the pressures and practical difficulties of life build, we may stray from whatever compassion we've been blessed to receive. Although we got the basic lessons and have experienced a taste of shared suffering or even a heavy dose, we find ways to prioritize other matters. We try to cover up a compassionate heart. If the pressure becomes too great, sadly, we may even succeed for a time.

Because compassion is at the root of kindness, right action, and good deeds, it also holds the promise of true peace. Following the path of Action means following a path of compassion. This requires not just acknowledgement and experience, but practice! We must pay attention to compassion — look where it points, follow where it leads — and let it guide our outlook and our actions. Make compassion a daily companion, and make loving-kindness a lifelong endeavor.

Wherever we are in our practice and our journey, just by acknowledging compassion, by giving it space in our lives and responding to it, we are throwing more fuel on the sacred fire. We are burning up our selfishness, our doubts, and our sense of separation and individuality. By embracing compassion, we work toward embracing everything.

Cultivating Love and Kindness

Love and kindness are widely associated with spirituality and the spiritual path. All those struggling on the path of Action are working to cultivate this love and kindness. When considering such a path, of course it sounds good, but how do we go about actually cultivating love and kindness?

Whatever love and kindness we're blessed with, through our personality, upbringing, and conditioning, is good. By all means, exercise what you've been gifted to the fullest. But if you wish to expand upon this, to grow the sphere of its influence in your life and the lives of others, if you wish to connect with a kind of loving-kindness that doesn't depend on personality, upbringing, or conditioning, then some kind of practice is usually needed.

Many prescribed techniques form the backbone of this kind of practice. To start with, we may need to *imagine* what greater love and kindness looks like and try to emulate that. We can bring up the love and kindness we already feel in a limited way and try to extend it toward others as we bring them into our awareness, even and especially those whom we despise or consider as enemies. We can inhale, noticing and acknowledging the suffering of others, and then exhale, radiating loving kindness.

More and more, we can pay attention to compassion in our lives and allow it to guide our thoughts and actions. Loving kindness is nothing less than compassion in action. We can practice by being watchful and sensitive to compassion in our daily lives. Then we can try to respond genuinely and seamlessly in our thoughts, words, and actions.

Anyone who undertakes such a practice seriously will quickly see it's not as easy as it sounds. The cruxes of the practice are "paying attention" and "responding genuinely and seamlessly." When first introduced to any practice, people have a tendency to approach it through the ego. *Okay, I'm going to do this!* In other words, they try to *make* themselves pay attention to compassion and try to *force* themselves to respond genuinely and seamlessly. Well, maybe you see the problem already.

Our attention is not really ours to command, nor is forced action ever seamless. Difficulty arises because we misidentify the source of our attention, our compassion, and our actions — and thus we don't really understand the source of loving kindness. When we think *I* can do it, we take the ego to be the source. But the actual situation is quite the opposite. The ego distracts from natural attention, obscures natural compassion, and interrupts natural action.

Try this as an experiment. Look at an object and think, *I am going to pay attention to this object.* In that moment, are you paying attention to it? Your attention is almost entirely on your thoughts — both the thought of *I* and the command to pay attention. The more you think about it, the less you do it. Now, let go of these thoughts, relax the mind, and just look. *Now* you see it. The less the ego is involved, the more clearly you see.

All spiritual practice requires the ego to be tamed, at least temporarily denied, and ultimately put in its proper place. Paying attention to compassion and cultivating loving kindness are not a matter of the ego being ever watchful or commanding various actions. The key is more a matter of letting go of the ego-self and all its views and ideas, hopes and fears, ambitions and doubts.

Compassion arises from reality itself, in which nothing is separate. Loving kindness is its natural work. All that's needed to follow this path is to get our egos out of the way. Just by getting our egos out of the way, we can unveil more loving kindness than our egos could possibly handle. So our practice has to start with calming and quieting the mind and body, and being at peace within ourselves. Then *innate* compassion can begin to find expression through us and do its work in our lives and the lives of others.

Practicing Charity and Free Giving

Of all the practices that lie in the path of Action, charity and free giving are perhaps the most straightforward. To share our time, to help others in need, and to give freely of our resources has an immediate impact on others, of course, but also on the giver.

The word *charity* these days is too often used to reference a particular cause or organization rather than charity itself. Of course, it's great to give to organizations working to benefit others. Such organization can do immense good and help many people. Donations are surely vital in that effort, and a tax break isn't bad, either. But if we focus too much on the organization and on getting something in return, we neglect our own practice of charity, no matter how much we give.

Charity is rooted in compassion, kindness, and free giving, without regard for personal gain. As a spiritual practice, it should reflect that. If our actions are rooted primarily in getting a tax break or appearing to do good, and only secondarily in helping others, it may be an intelligent use of our money and even a great benefit to the world, but it's superficial as spiritual practice.

For this reason, our practice of charity cannot be measured in time, money, or material goods. What matters is the internal states from which our actions arise and the internal states our actions, in turn, cultivate. For this reason, when it comes to spiritual practice, a generous heart, a simple act, even a gaze or a smile well-placed, can be far greater than a million-dollar charitable donation.

Of course, as in all practices, we have to start somewhere. We may have to convince ourselves, or even force ourselves, to give our time, attention, money, or help to others. That's okay. By all means, do it. Giving can be a gesture toward letting go. In performing all such gestures, set your intention on cultivating selflessness and non-attachment.

As our practice continues, we should look to develop an attitude toward charity and free giving that flows seamlessly from innate compassion. In this way, our charity is a manifestation of the loving kindness that encompasses all beings.

Following Precepts

A common theme on the path of Action is following precepts, a set of rules or aspirations guiding thoughts and behavior. Using precepts is so common we may not think about it as practice, but it most certainly is. The precepts serve to challenge our selfish views and put our everyday actions in accord with our highest spiritual ideals.

Precepts can be adopted directly from an appropriate tradition or tailored to your specific needs. Either way, they should be contemplated and taken on as a reflection of our highest ideals. Whether they represent various "right actions" or "shall nots," precepts are followed with the intention of aligning the body, mind, and spirit. Insofar as we're successful, we ward off, avoid, and dissolve obstacles to real insight, real peace, and real happiness.

Many people don't like being told what to do or not do. But that's missing the point. Think of precepts as telling *yourself* how to avoid trouble and obstacles, and helping you to behave in a manner conducive to your goals. Following precepts reflects your highest ideals, your innate compassion, your love and kindness, and your desire for the truth.

It's not always easy, but the struggle to follow the precepts — to remember them and apply them to your life — is part of the practice. It's a good idea to recite your precepts regularly. That way, they will be in the forefront of your mind, and ready to apply in difficult situations.

The conditioned body and mind have ingrained reactions that take on a direction and momentum all their own. Sometimes we have gotten into some bad habits … and sometimes we've gotten into a deep mess because of them. Taking on precepts and working to follow them is a way of setting our intention to clean things up and to let go of selfish views.

If you commit to following a set of good precepts, consistently applying them to your actions and the situations you encounter, real transformation is possible. You may struggle and fail many times to live up to your precepts fully. But if you keep practicing, you will find you don't stumble as much, you get yourself into less trouble, you have fewer problems and anxieties, and you have more time and energy to devote to your spiritual path.

If you consistently put forth sincere effort to follow a set of well-chosen precepts, real change can work its way into your mind and body. You will begin to see things differently. If you persist in the practice, you may experience a clarity in action you never thought possible.

The Trap of Hypocrisy

On the path of Action, hypocrisy is the most formidable trap. Let's assume we've already moved beyond unrepentant evil, and are at least making an effort toward right action. Hypocrisy can then appear in two forms. In one form, we profess right action, but nevertheless do things we know to be wrong. In the other form, we actually go through all the motions of right action, but it's just a show, and our hearts remain unchanged.

Both forms of hypocrisy hinge around creating a mask of righteousness. While we may say kind words or appear to do good, it's just an act that conceals selfish desires and gives cover to cherished delusions. There's a disconnect between our stated ideals and our actions or our actions and our thoughts.

On this path of Action, some form or level of hypocrisy, however minor, is inevitable. The whole point of the path is making an effort, trying to change, attempting to transform yourself. In this situation, if we're honest, some degree of hypocrisy always appears. That's okay, as long as we keep putting effort into practice and avoid falling into cynicism.

Hopefully, you can see that conceptualization, idolatry, and hypocrisy are, in some ways, very similar traps. Each trap involves mistaking a representation for the reality. Each, in its way, mistakes a pointing finger for the radiance of the moon. Practice points us toward reality, but reality itself transcends all representations.

When on the path of Action — cultivating compassion, doing good deeds, trying to give freely, struggling with desires, bad habits, and so on — it's normal to encounter failure. Again and again in our practice, we will fall short of perfection. That's only natural, as long as we're practicing on the path. If you're not encountering failure occasionally, your goals are not high enough or you're not practicing sincerely.

Please remember, you will never achieve perfection through the ego, because it's not the source of our actions. Our behavior cannot be righted by willpower or force. All such attempts will only entangle us further. But the more we let go of the ego-self, seeing through its delusions of power, then the higher power can begin to work seamlessly in our lives.

Putting Action into Practice

Whoever you are, whatever your background, whatever your religion and particular beliefs or non-beliefs, there's always room on the path for doing good deeds, freely giving, and putting kindness into action. Whoever we are in this world, and no matter how far we've gone astray or wandered off course, we're all called to this path of Action. Anyone can make an effort to put this path into practice.

All it takes is some sense of kindness and compassion combined with mindfulness of the situations we find ourselves in. This is a most elemental and streamlined practice, directly related to our lives as they are, and to events and situation as they appear every day.

Stop thinking about yourself so much. Stop feeling sorry for yourself or trying to build yourself up or be somebody important. Just take a look around you and notice the needs, concerns, worries, fears, and troubles of others.

Ask yourself: *What can I do to put kindness into action? What can I do to help improve this situation?*

To help break the shell, challenge yourself to charitable actions you might not usually undertake. Volunteer to help others, feed the hungry, care for the sick, comfort the dying, assist the unfortunate. Take yourself a little out of your comfort zone. It's good practice!

Keep in mind, though, this ongoing practice doesn't have to be monumental. You don't have to save the world. Leave that to the higher power. Just be attentive to what you can do in the moment. The smallest kindnesses in the context of everyday life — just a smile, gesture, or unasked favor — can constitute a profound practice when applied with consistency.

Be attentive and look for opportunities to put your kindness into practice. Don't seek any gain. There is nothing to gain. Just give. Look for opportunities to see what you're holding onto, and let it go through acts of kindness, compassion, and free giving.

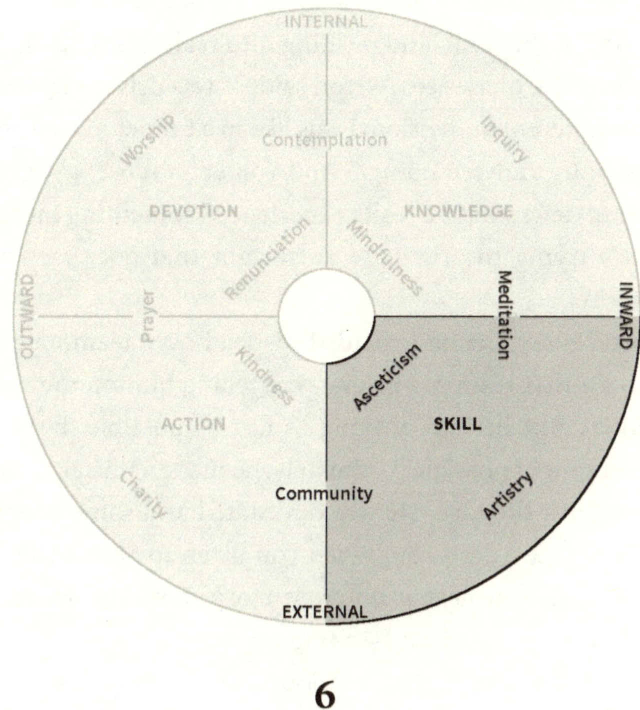

6

PATH OF SKILL

In the 1988 Monaco Grand Prix qualifiers, Ayrton Senna drove what is widely regarded as the greatest lap in the history of Formula One racing. As Senna drove his McLaren-Honda MP4/4 through the winding streets of Monaco with 1200 horsepower of turbo-charged fury screaming behind his back, something extraordinary happened. And this happening — a kind of transcendence — could only happen because of Senna's obsession not just with winning, but driving at the limit, and pushing into realms unknown.

About the experience, Ayrton said, "I was driving by instinct. I was in a different dimension. I was like in a tunnel ... well beyond my conscious understanding." And you get a sense, if you listen to the interviews, that he really experienced something inexpressible. He's trying to articulate an insight that goes far beyond motorsports.

On race day, Senna extended his lead over teammate Alain Prost so far that team managers were telling him on the radio to slow down. But he kept driving as fast as possible, faster than anybody thought possible. Ultimately, he made a mistake, ran into a wall and lost the race. He was devastated and some people say he threw the race away, but when you listen to Senna talk about that weekend, you hear a different story. It's clear he touched something far greater than winning a race.

Skill, when very highly developed and relentlessly pursued, can become a path to truth itself. For within the search for deeper and more profound levels of ability, one must eventually go beyond the ego-self. Every fear, doubt, and emotion, every hope, ambition, and thought that may hold us back, has to be let go. A process of self-objectification in pursuit of a higher goal — of facing, examining, and optimizing every aspect of the body-mind, and of pushing ourselves to and beyond previously imagined limits — provides real opportunities for insight and transcendence.

We don't have to be Formula One drivers or top-tier athletes to pursue this path of Skill. But we do have to push beyond our previously-imagined limitations. There are many accounts of martial arts masters who found awakening beyond the heights of their greatest achievements. There are alpinists who have encountered profundity within their dangerous feats. There are actors, musicians, and artists who are ever aiming at perfection through art. There are those who practice making and serving tea with transcendent precision. There are surgeons who revel in the power to save lives. All are on a path of Skill.

Those who are attracted to developing *any* skill are already on this path. But the spiritual dimension comes to bear when our effort to surpass prior limits necessitates a deeper examination of self. When our effort to develop a skill becomes simultaneously an effort to plumb the mysteries of existence, then our practice necessarily becomes spiritual, whether we know it or not.

Whenever we challenge ourselves, pushing our abilities to the limit and beyond, we are throwing wood on the sacred fire. We are challenging not just our conditioned skill, but our very conceptions of ourselves and our limitations. Again and again, like a moth we fly close to the flames, singeing and burning off bits and pieces of ourselves. If we're determined in our efforts, eventually we may fly right into the fire.

The Importance of Desire

Many spiritual traditions warn against the dangers of desire. Some go as far as to say desire is the root of suffering. While this may be right from one point of view, from another point of view it's misleading. Certain kinds of desire can be very helpful, even essential, for our spiritual practice.

Consider why we set off on a spiritual path to begin with. Why would we even light this sacred fire? Something serves as a catalyst, and that something is very likely desire. But this desire is of an unusual sort. Although it takes various outward forms, it's not essentially a desire for anything in particular. Rather, it's a longing for truth, for reality, for authenticity, for satisfaction, and for an end to suffering.

Even in the case of a person who goes off determined to become a monk or a sadhu, with the intention of eliminating desire, they do so out of desire. It may seem paradoxical, but I don't think it is. This desire is really a will to the ultimate truth, a determination to know oneself completely, a longing for God alone. This desire is essential on the path! It's the very fire that consumes all other desires, all limited concepts, and all selfish beliefs.

On the path of Skill, this fundamental desire manifests through a desire for skill acquisition and mastery. Of course, on the path we don't necessarily think like that, but nevertheless the desire to achieve *something* through skill is a reflection of this deeper desire.

Practicing a skill is a way to, at least, try to approach what we intuitively desire but don't really know and can't really express.

At the beginning of the path, we may be just attracted to the particular aesthetics and imagined experience or utility of a particular skill. When we commit to a practice the attraction grows, but sooner or later struggles appear. For our practice to continue, we must have a desire and determination to unravel its deepest mysteries, despite all obstacles, and achieve our greatest potential.

If followed sincerely, honestly, and doggedly, such determination eventually and inevitably leads us to the disillusionment of false ideas, direct inquiry into ourselves, and an encounter with fundamental emptiness. Provided we avoid or get past the various traps set in our way, the end of the path reveals a truth far greater than any particular activity, achievement, or skill. It reveals the truth of oneself and reality itself.

Creative Endeavors

The artful creation of words, objects, images, and events as expressions of thoughts, memories, and emotions is valued by virtually all cultures. Accomplished artists are often regarded with a measure of admiration. What is at the heart of this? Appreciation for the aesthetics of the creation is one factor, but the mystery of creation itself and the evocation of thought, memory, beauty, emotion, introspection, insight, and intuition is what gives art real impact.

On the path of Skill, the artist is a kind of explorer, plumbing the depths of the creative ability, drawing on their sense perception and experience. There's such incredible depth to the human experience! Can those depths be expressed through artistic creation? Can they be recreated? Shown? Shared? And what does it mean to experience such wonder through art? Questions like these are the purview of those on the path.

From ancient times, storytelling, painting, music, and dancing have embodied this creative path. Like a magician, the artist both recreates the world through representation and creates a fresh new experience in the world. To capture hearts, minds, and imaginations in an almost religious-like wonder has always been part of that endeavor. But for the artist, the work is rooted in an exploration of their direct experience.

In modern times, the angst of the struggling artist has become a common trope. At its worst, such angst merely reflects a selfish frustration with unfulfilled egoic desires — for recognition, fame, money, and so on. At its best, at its most noble, this angst reflects a yearning for perfection and for the ultimate expression — to bring into the world our deepest, most profound experience, our most authentic being, and love itself. Either way, the artist's struggle is a reflection of that fundamental frustration, what Buddhism calls *dukkha,* which is potent fuel for our sacred fire.

From a spiritual perspective, an artist begins by just trying to develop the skill to create something pleasing and well-crafted, or that reflects admirable qualities. But what we find pleasing, why something is well-crafted, and the ephemeral, inexpressible qualities we admire in great art, are not trivial matters. They go to the very heart of why pursuit of such skill can be regarded as a spiritual path. Whether consciously or not, the artist sets their sights on truth. They may yet peer through a long kaleidoscope, enchanted by shapes and colors, but the light beyond shines brightly and illuminates all.

Mind-Body Practices

Coordination of the mind and body via athletics, dance, martial arts, et cetera, can also become a spiritual practice. Whether we seek peak performance in a sport, technical mastery in a body-focused art, or true union through yoga, all such endeavors, at the extreme, lead to direct inquiry into the self. Even the casual athlete who attempts to improve is already on the path, although only at the very beginning. By following this path beyond the mere performance of higher and higher levels of skill, the spiritual nature of all such endeavors comes to bear.

Yoga is perhaps the obvious example here. At least traditionally, its stated goal is "union" or enlightenment, although modern styles of yoga may not directly address the spiritual dimension. We might have a vague feeling or aspiration of doing something spiritual, but the actual path unfolds only through consistent, dedicated practice. Whether the practice is overtly spiritual or not, we still have to walk the path.

Some may view the acquisition of physical skill as a selfish endeavor, focused on self-improvement and personal gain. While this may be true in the beginning, it's somewhat true for the beginning of all paths and practices. If we're really drawn to physical practice, to be dissuaded by this notion would be short sighted, and could delay our actual path. We may only reach our limits through extensive physical practice. Only by pressing forward can the karmic forces at work in our lives run their course and be exhausted, and only then will our true selfless nature be revealed.

With regard to sports, we're generally looking to learn, improve, and find peak performance. This is especially true for any competitive sport, as the very nature of competition places a high value on winning. There's nothing wrong with seeking optimal performance, but as long as we're seeking to achieve or maintain it, even at high levels, we're still struggling with clarification. It's not until we let go of endless improvement and winning, through a natural culmination of performance-based desires or by coming up against our psycho-physical limitations that the spiritual dimension of practice comes into focus.

For decades, I trained in martial arts. Although I trained in non-sport martial arts, there was still a drive to achieve better performance, martial efficacy, and deeper understanding. Extensive experience led to gains on all fronts, but I always felt there were missing pieces. So I kept searching, through more training, novel approaches, new teachers, and different arts. When the missing pieces finally fell into place, it wasn't really how, why, or what I expected. Although I had achieved my superficial goals, I felt disillusioned. I kept training and teaching, even though, to some extent, I had stopped trying to improve. Now I would say that's precisely when the spiritual aspect of training came into play, and deeper insight began to emerge. Of course, I didn't recognize it at the time, but the actuality of that path is undeniable now.

So while, as in all paths, we begin with some desires, these desires are an important component of the spiritual journey. On the path of Skill, the desire to develop the body-mind toward high ideals, particular ends and achievements, or even just winning may be a driving force at the beginning. But those desires change with dedicated practice and we are ultimately disillusioned of them. If we're persistent and continue with practice through various plateaus and disillusionments, our insights will deepen, and we will become more and more open to the way of selflessness.

What is Mastery?

Within the path of Skill, there's usually a sense of aiming at continual improvement and exploration. The beginner may imagine that at some point in the future, they will master a skill and thereby bring their work to completion. But *true* mastery is something else entirely.

As practitioners on the path, we should understand that perfection cannot be attained through the body or mind. Even while we strive toward higher levels of skill, greater achievements, continual improvement and exploration, we should know this cycle is potentially unending, and sooner or later the body will fail and the mind will decline. At some point, this very knowledge gives proper perspective to the pursuit of skill as a spiritual path.

The beginning of the path is well trodden, and many have traveled toward improvement and higher levels of skill, their fires fueled by desires for ability, recognition, and achievement. But when their desires cannot be fully satisfied in one way or another, most stop walking or let the fire die out. Perhaps they run up against physical or psychological limitations. Perhaps they glimpse the emptiness of their desires. Only a few will continue on, will keep practicing, even when desire falters. To keep the fires going, they will now need to throw bits and pieces of *themselves* into the flames.

The continuing path to mastery can be understood as progressing through harmonizing of body, mind, and world to merging with the seamless and spontaneous flow of phenomena. At each step, the practitioner lets go of more and more of themselves and trusts more and more in that spontaneous flow.

So true mastery requires something more than just a super-high level of skill. On the one hand, there are some who attain a super-high level of skill, but cannot be considered true masters. Why is that? What's missing? On the other hand, there are those whose skill is waning and yet undoubtedly remain masters of their art. Why? No matter how high the level of skill, true mastery requires the transcendence of personal desires. This alone imparts the kind of freedom which is the hallmark of masters.

The Trap of Egotism

The greatest trap on the path of Skill is egotism — an exaggerated sense of self-importance that arises from a strong belief in the ego-self as the doer of actions and possessor of skills. Those who become trapped in this view will not move beyond the desires of the ego. At some point, this will hamper skill development. While it's possible in many practices to reach extremely high levels of skill while still being trapped in egotism — some may even become ego maniacs — with regard to the spiritual path, it remains a trap.

Egotism, like the traps of other paths, relies on fundamental mistakes we have already made at the beginning of our journey. Here, we've mistaken the ego-self as the source of our actions and the receptacle of our powers and abilities. Because we have this view already when we set out on the path, some measure of egotism is inevitable. In fact, a big part of the path is uncovering our mistakes and moving beyond this view.

A measure of egoic desire is normal, and even essential, on the path — desire for skill, accomplishments, and even mastery. But those who make progress, fulfilling at least some of their desires, are at risk of developing too much pride. Like a poison, pride swells and distorts the ego, obscuring any potential insight.

So how are we to avoid, or at least minimize, this trap of egotism?

Some corrective mechanisms are built into the pursuit of various skills. The chess player's pride may be kept in check by the occasional loss or the fact that they cannot beat the best chess computers. In fact, all competitive sports have the potential for losses, and that's a great blessing. In mountaineering, there are life-threatening dangers, like storms, avalanches, crevasses, and potentially impossible routes, which are a constant reminder of the ego's limitations. For the artist, the inability to perfectly create an envisioned masterpiece can be a good reality check, painful as it may be.

All failures temper the ego, and we are almost always better off for having had them. Losses are as important as wins; failure is as important as success. By cultivating humility and empathetic joy, we can ensure we make the most of all aspects of our practice. The more we understand and remind ourselves improvement doesn't happen because of the ego, but rather because of practice itself, and skill does not reside in the ego, but rather in reality itself, the better situated we are to avoid the trap of egotism and approach our practice as a spiritual path.

The path is not a matter of acquisition, but rather a path of transformation through letting go. Egotism will stymie our practice at higher levels due to over reliance on egoic direction. This often crops up in the form of the old getting-in-our-own-way problem or the over-thinking problem or the loss-of-confidence problem. These problems, in and of themselves, are pointing the way beyond the ego-self. They are prompting us to let go.

Putting Skill into Practice

We don't have to be world-class athletes or genius-level artists to pursue the path of Skill. In some area of our lives, we may already be on it. All those who seek to improve the performance of some action are already on this path. So let's look at how anybody can pursue skill as a spiritual practice.

Select an area of skill to pursue. Perhaps you play music, draw, or paint. Perhaps you would like to learn another language or how to cook pastries. Maybe you just want to get better at doing the dishes. Whatever it is can be an approach to practice. Pick something you can commit to going deeply into. It doesn't really matter what it is, so much as your intention to practice as a path of spiritual discovery.

Practice regularly and be attentive to the process. You will go through the same difficulties meditators have, such as developing focus, overcoming expectations, impatience, ambition, boredom, frustration, and self doubt in order to persevere in your practice. This perseverance alone will teach you many things.

Observe what works and what doesn't, what makes results better or worse, and how to make substantial progress in developing a skill. You will need to study whatever teachings are available on the subject, and you may need to seek out a teacher, or many teachers, along the way.

When you encounter obstacles to continued improvement, you have to ask yourself how to overcome them. You have to analyze what's going on, what's the real obstacle, what don't you understand, what's really holding you back. Don't worry about how objectively "good" you are. Just keep asking questions, keep discovering, and keep practicing.

Perhaps the most important question you can ask yourself throughout this process is how you're standing in your own way. In other words, in what way are "you" holding back your own progress and ability, and how can you get out of the way. Just as an example, how can you let go of self-doubt or frustration in order to allow the process of practice to do its work? Because ultimately, as with all other paths and practices, *letting go* is the key to better practice and deeper insight.

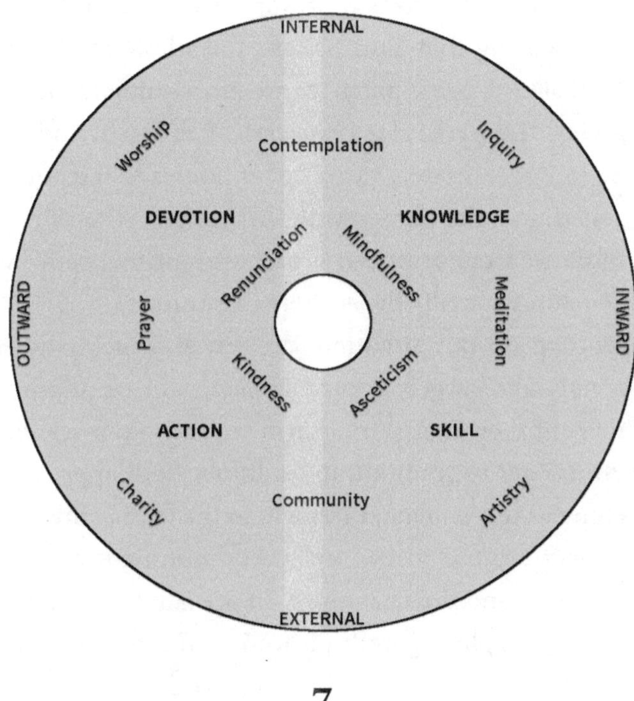

7

ALL PATHS ARE THE SAME PATH

On the spiritual journey, all paths are ultimately the same path. Knowledge, Devotion, Action, and Skill are like a golden braid. They are interwoven and converge on the same truth. The details of practices and individual lives vary widely, but whatever the details, all spiritual practices eventually lead to selflessness and Realization.

Spiritual practice directs us toward truth and challenges the obstacles obscuring that truth. That's the whole matter, simply stated. To that end, some practices are more suitable than others for removing the particular obstacles of different individuals. Karmic forces necessitate a variety of antidotes to the poisons we have ingested, so we're blessed with that variety. Almost anything could be followed and practiced as part of a spiritual path, because the whole path is actually the entirety of our lives.

Depending on our situation, desires, and inclinations, our practice may land largely rooted in one path or another, one tradition or another … or we may drift around in our search, from teacher to teacher or tradition to tradition. Both approaches are valid, as long as we remember our will to the truth, and as long as we don't drift around just to avoid commitment, clarification, disillusionment, and direct inquiry. In actuality, the path of our life often has us exploring multiple leads and directions at once.

No matter your approach, what really matters is not necessarily choosing the right practice, right tradition, or right teacher, but at every moment engaging wholeheartedly with whatever practice appears in the context of your life. If we knew how to unravel our lives and the obstacles that stand in the way of illumination, peace, and true happiness, we would do it. The reality is that we can only unravel our lives and dispel these obstacles by following the path wherever *it* leads.

Don't be afraid of mistakes. What we think of as mistakes are guaranteed. Of course, do your best and be discerning. Try to find good teachers, good teachings, and good practices. But everything is self correcting. If you make a wrong turn, as long as you're earnest in your efforts and set your sights on the highest possible outcomes, you will eventually turn back in the right direction.

We cannot expect to understand a teaching or a practice at the outset. We have to do the work and walk the path. So the most important attributes when approaching practice are intention, earnestness, and effort. Set your intentions high, however impossible or improbable your goals may seem. We may not know what ultimate truth is or looks like, but we should fully intend to find out. Avoid cynicism and cultivate a sincere earnestness in your practice. Finally, put in the effort. Only you can do the work, and only you can find out who you truly are.

All Traps are the Same Trap

For each of the four paths, we've identified a principal trap: Conceptualism, Idolatry, Hypocrisy, and Egotism. These traps and associated obstacles can map onto a mandala just like the four paths and associated practices. Within Conceptualism, we find sophistry and cynicism. Within Idolatry, we find nihilism and fanaticism. Within Hypocrisy, we find dishonesty and deception. Within Egotism, we find pride and egomania. In-between the primary traps are obstacles like fundamentalism, behaviorism, greed, and solipsism.

In our discussion, however, we also showed how all the traps are really just variations on a theme. So actually, all these traps are the same trap. That being the case, we should firmly understand what that trap is on a more fundamental level.

As practitioners, we may drift between and through the different paths on our spiritual journey, driven by the karmic forces at work in our lives. With each new practice, we encounter new excitement, new challenges, and seemingly new obstacles. This all serves to keep us spinning our wheels and never fully transcending any obstacle or practice. Fundamentally, we keep falling into the same trap and keep failing to find our way out.

On my journey, I ventured into every path at some point and tried many practices, wandering in the wilderness, searching for a clarity that always seemed stubbornly elusive. I was driven first by desire, then by frustration, then by desperation, and finally by resolve. I faced all the traps we have mentioned, and some we haven't. In retrospect, there was really only one obstacle, and that was *myself* — a tangle of shifting beliefs and ideas that was always at the center of the circus.

If we're earnest in our endeavors, the traps of conceptualism, idolatry, hypocrisy, and egotism are inevitable along the way. These obstacles are baked into the journey from the very beginning, arising from the same fundamental mistake that put us on the journey to begin with. I say "mistake," but it's just phenomena, the play of consciousness. It's only a mistake with regard to recognizing the truth. Things arise which we identify with, and although these things are not fundamentally real, we have taken them to be so.

All the traps and obstacles we encounter on the path are formulations of this initial mistake. Conceptualism, Idolatry,

Hypocrisy, and Egotism are different ways of putting some *thing* in place of reality. Whether that thing is a conceptual understanding, a golden calf, a mask of righteousness, or an idea of oneself, the mistake and the obstacle are essentially the same.

Whatever the particular formulation, the crux of the problem is always oneself, because it's the first thing we have taken to be real. All other mistakes are supported by this one, so the direction of all the paths must go through this *self.* Transcending the ego-self is the main prerequisite to realization.

All Ends are the Same End

However steadfast or circuitous our route, however long or short, and wherever we venture among the various paths and practices, the ultimate end is the same end. Just as all paths are really one path and all traps are really one trap, all ends are really one end. While our stated goal, depending on the details of our path, may be something like truth, God, true love, or self-mastery, the real goal transcends everything, including all prior understanding, thoughts, and goals.

All practices eventually require self emptying. That is the unifying principle of the spiritual path. At some point, if all external, projected, and superficial obstacles are clarified, removed, set aside, successfully negotiated, or moved past, and yet we persist … no matter the path or the practice, we will come to this real crux of the matter.

It may seem like a long way down the path or it may be staring you right in the face, but sooner or later we have to deal with ourselves. We have to encounter ourselves as the primary obstacle, as the creator of all our problems, hang-ups, and troubles. We have to see this tangle of thoughts and dreams, hopes and fears, beliefs and desires for what it is … and what it isn't.

Seeing the ego-self for what it is may come with spontaneous insight into what lies beyond. If it doesn't bring full recognition, at least we know from which direction the light is shining. If we continue our practice, we may now begin to take pieces of that ego-self and throw them into the sacred fire. Take anything and everything that is not real and absolutely true … and throw it into the fire.

When everything that is unreal and untrue has been burned up, when the fuel is gone and the flames have died down to a flicker, at any moment, with a gust of wind, a shift of air, or a collapse of burnt wood, the fire may, of its own accord, blow out. A bed of coals may yet glow. Wisps of smoke may linger a while, but *your* practice has come to an end.

PART THREE

WALKING THE PATH

Wherein we discuss topics relevant to navigating practice on the spiritual path.

8

THE BIG PICTURE

Q: How can we understand the overall course and direction of practice?

A: You can't, not really. Your actual journey can only be known by going through it. However, it can be helpful to have some idea where you're going and how to get there. It's only an idea, but it can still be helpful.

Aiming toward Transcendence

When we consider a practice, we usually think about learning, doing, and getting good at it. That's perfectly fine at the outset, but spiritual practice is an unusual endeavor. Not only can it take almost any form, but it aims at transcending itself. So our real destination is not doing or getting good at the thing, but rather transcending the thing — and indeed *all* things.

Of course, we have to do the work. I'm not suggesting we can forgo practice altogether. We should not expect transcendence without actually walking the path. One way or another, we have to bring ourselves to the threshold of awakening through conscious or unconscious practice. But to have a clear view of practice, we should understand that the highest level includes transcending practice itself.

Perhaps we should talk a little about this word: *transcend*. The definition is "to go beyond the limits of." This is good, but in the spiritual context, there's a deeper sense. It's not just going beyond level 1 or 2 or 108, or any definable limit. It's going beyond distinctions, levels, and limits altogether. This type of transcendence can be likened to "letting go" or "equanimity" or "high indifference." We don't have to leave practice in order to transcend, it's rather that "practice" and "no practice" becomes one and the same.

We may start a meditation practice and "do" our meditation once or twice a day. While meditating, we work to calm the body-mind, observe phenomena, and go into "meditative" states. This is all much-needed practice. But if we transcend, it no longer makes any difference whether we meditate or not. Without any distinctions, we are always in the stateless state.

Let's not get ahead of ourselves, though. We're here to discuss practice, not enlightenment. So let's stick with understanding why it's important to have this aim of transcendence in your practice when, even to have a hope of getting there, we just have to throw ourselves into the practice anyway.

Aiming for transcendence reminds us that we cannot hold on to anything. While our practice can be an aid to letting go, clinging even to the form of practice becomes, at some point, an obstacle itself — a form of idolatry, really.

Dedicated practice is like putting all your eggs in one basket. In practical matters this usually isn't a good idea, but in spiritual practice, it's a sound method. In mantra practice, for example, we repeat the mantra until it folds everything into itself. We can think of spiritual practice as working to put everything into that one basket. Don't forget to put yourself and the basket itself in! Then, instead of dropping ten-thousand things, we need only set down our basket.

Universal Practices

When recommending practices, I lean toward meditation and self-inquiry, and I often use them when answering general questions about practice. Perhaps one reason is that meditation and self-inquiry were central to my path. Of course, I engaged in many other practices, from martial arts to religious worship, but elements of meditation and self-inquiry were always involved. For one reason or another, many practices are not suitable for everyone. Martial arts, for example, is really only suitable to a small number of people, religion isn't generally suitable for avowed atheists, et cetera. Meditation and self-inquiry, however, can be taken up by just about anyone.

To be clear, everyone must discover their own path, and there will be many twists and turns. Many different practices may be involved, in serial, in parallel, or in concert. But a case can be made for meditation and self-inquiry as universal practices. Not only can anyone take them up, but they're readily integrated into any other type of practice. So whatever our religion or worldview, and whatever other practices we engage in, there's always room for meditation and self-inquiry.

What are the strengths of these practices and why can they be considered universal? There are three related and interconnected factors.

First, these practices contain very little, if any, content with regard to a worldview. In the West, meditation is most often associated with Buddhism, but nothing about the essence of meditation makes it a Buddhist practice. Meditation was practiced long before Buddhism and anybody can do it without becoming a Buddhist or believing anything in particular. Likewise, while self-inquiry — *atma vichara* — may be associated with Hindu traditions, nothing about the practice presupposes adherence to any idea. In fact, the practice is asking you to go beyond ideas and directly investigate through experience.

Second, these practices are extremely minimalistic. Not only are they not bogged down by weighty worldviews, but the instructions are also very simple. Meditation, for example, could be regarded as just paying attention. Although there are many types of meditation with specific instructions, implied inquiries, and guided experiences, the essence of the practice is just open awareness, without grasping or resistance. Many meditation techniques are just a method for getting to that. Likewise, in self-inquiry, the whole of the practice can be summed up by the question "Who am I?" and seeking the source or true nature of the self directly.

Anybody can take up these practices. Regardless of worldview, past experience, or physical ability, pretty much everyone can pay attention and inquire into the nature of self. Age, intellect, education, religious views, cultural background, socio-economic status, all matter very little when it comes to these practices. To focus, to develop concentration, and to watch and observe what's happening within our experience is a straight-forward task. So is asking a basic question like "Who am I?" with the intention of truly knowing the self. It doesn't matter what else we're doing. We can always pay attention and ask, "Who is doing this?"

The third and final factor which suggests these practices are universal is they go right to the heart of matter. Many practices provide too many opportunities to get lost in the weeds, to go further into delusion rather than out of it, to get distracted by new ideas, new concepts, new abilities, and new views. Because meditation and self-inquiry are so minimalistic, these practices allow fewer avenues for escape or distraction. The work may seem difficult, but it's clear. Whatever path we take, awareness is the vehicle of our journey, and the way inevitably passes through the self.

On Asceticism

When we think of asceticism, we usually go straight to the extremes. We imagine medieval monks donning hair shirts and waking in the middle of the night to pray, wild-eyed mystics dwelling deep in the desert, emaciated meditators fasting in the forest for weeks on end, hermits dwelling in mountain caves, or naked sadhus smearing their bodies with ash from a sacred fire. But actually, all spiritual practice contains an element of asceticism. It may be relatively minor when compared to extreme feats of ascetic practice, but the element is there.

The word *asceticism* comes from a Greek word meaning "training" or "practice," and was originally associated with athletics. Later it became associated with rigorous spiritual practices found in traditions worldwide. Now it tends to refer to abstinence from pleasures and indulgences, or perhaps more succinctly, self-denial. In other words, asceticism is an undermining of the ego-self and its desires, impulses, and tendencies. In meditation, for example, when we feel an itch and refrain from scratching, that's asceticism.

In the broadest view, asceticism is one and the same with spiritual practice. It may go from mild to extreme, but nevertheless it's central to the program. That's not always clear from the beginning because we think, I *want* to do this. But all practices involve discipline, and if you get into any practice far enough, it will require some level of self-denial. Eventually, that becomes the whole point. We practice in order to transcend the ego-self and recognize our true all-encompassing nature. Again, the way is selflessness.

Meditation, for example, restrains the self by denying it activity. You just have to sit there. Restlessness, distractions, thoughts, et cetera, are all symptoms of an ego-self that doesn't care to be restrained. So we practice in order to tame it, calm it down, and see it for what it is.

Religious devotion, for example, restrains the self by imposing disciplines of time and place, word and deed. At these times, on this schedule, we worship. We do these specific things. We say these specific words. We don't eat these foods. We don't do these things.

Charity, for example, restrains the self by giving to others what we might otherwise use for ourselves — our time, money, thoughts, or consideration. Instead of acting for our own benefit, we act for the benefit of others. We put aside our own concerns in favor of helping others.

Art, for example, restrains the self by requiring time, effort, sacrifice, and going beyond self consciousness, self doubt, and self criticism. Although many artists may be mired in the ego, the highest achievements always require transcendence of self.

The Buddha called his teachings the middle way. Although he practiced extreme asceticism in his own journey, he maintained that such extremes were not necessary. But some — a middling amount — is still necessary. That's why he taught meditation and gave precepts for students to follow. To be clear, he was still recommending some level of asceticism, but we need not go to extremes.

We don't need to starve ourselves, but practicing some restraint is helpful. We don't need to stare at a wall for nine years, but consistent meditation is helpful. We don't need to give away all our money and possessions, but freely giving is helpful. What really matters is letting go of attachment.

Of course, each individual path is unique, and each journey unfolds according to karmic forces. Some people, for one reason or another, may still need to go to some extremes, due to stubbornness, past trauma, excessive ambition, crazy ideas, and so on. But when not absolutely necessary, if we're sensitive and really pay attention, we can learn everything we need from just a moderate level of asceticism.

The Old Bait and Switch

All sincere teaching, given in good faith, is a kind of bait and switch. This sounds bad, like somebody is trying to deceive you, but it's really the opposite. The bait and switch is necessary and not even of the teacher's making. Not only is it for the student's benefit, but also according to and provided by the student's own beliefs and misunderstandings. There really isn't any other way for teaching to happen.

Think about it. If the student already knew what the teacher knew, why would they go to them for instruction? There would be no need or desire. On the other hand, if the student didn't *believe* the teacher knows something they don't, they also wouldn't seek out instruction. So the student has some kind of idea in mind of what the teachers knows, but they themselves don't really know it. To them, it's just an idea, and inevitably a mistaken one.

So the student's own mistaken ideas, misunderstandings, fantasies, and deluded ambitions provide the bait. The teacher's task is to disillusion the student of all these thoughts and introduce them to fundamental emptiness. The good teacher does not replace one delusion with another. Rather, true knowledge is simply revealed in the absence of delusion.

In martial arts, for example, a student typically comes in with a wide range of ideas. Many have fantasies in mind, fueled by movies and television. Others have ambitions of becoming a badass or a master. Some just want to be able to defend themselves, should the need arise. They're the most sensible lot, but they too have certain deluded ideas. None of them, of course, know what they're truly in for. They will only find out through dedicated practice and training — through Focusing, Observing, Manipulating, and Emptying.

Progress doesn't happen all at once. After a year of practice, the student may say "Wow, I really didn't understand anything about this when I started," as if that's a surprise to them. They've gotten a taste of disillusionment, but probably they have a whole new set of ideas, based on what they've done and the insights they've had.

Consider the following abstract illustration: At the beginning, you're taught the first principle. You practice that for while until you basically know it. Then you're taught the second principle and practice that for while until you have some understanding of it. When you go back to the first principle, you realize you didn't really know it at all. It's completely different now, in the context of second-principle knowledge! So you start again learning the first and second principle, and then you're given the third principle. Again, when you go back to the first and second principle, your understanding is completely different. And so it progresses, always circling around to deeper understanding.

This bait and switch of the teaching, this process of disillusionment, happens throughout our journey. It's the old bait and switch from bottom to top, from beginner to master. Is there anything to really learn? You may develop skill, of course, or even a deep understanding, and I don't want to demean that in any way. Skill and understanding are very helpful in this world, but progress itself is empty. Of course, keep going! Don't stop. But ask yourself, in whatever practice you follow, in light of a potentially endless process, what could ultimate wisdom really look like?

Inquire into Everything

Although we may have a dedicated time for spiritual practice, every situation and moment is ripe for inquiry. Any choice, thought, action, sensation, emotion, event, or object can serve as a seed for our inquiry. Absolutely everything is an opportunity to ask "What is happening?" and "Who is experiencing this?" Everything being some part or manifestation of reality, there is no shortage of opportunities to look deeper.

Ultimately, I have no interest in discussing the merits of various philosophies, systems, techniques, or schools of practice. These things are only there as an aid to our inquiry. That's great, but it's your actual inquiry that matters, not the particulars of your approach.

In Yoga, for example, the movement, the breath, the struggles, and the calm are all there to stimulate looking within. So many experiences and contrasts are ripe for insight in one who *really* looks. The disposition and effort of the practitioner is far more important than the specifics of the practice when it comes to clarification and insight.

At the beginning of any practice, a desire to learn forms and master technical elements is natural. That's fine, and can be beneficial. But to go deeper, observe not just the superficial aspects of experience, but also the inner workings. Inquire into sensations, emotional states, thoughts, doubts, hopes, and fears, with the purpose of understanding oneself. And endeavor to practice emptying by letting go of these same sensations, emotions, thoughts, doubts, hopes, and fears.

Inquiry is not limited to formal practice. It can and should spread through the whole of our lives. Pay attention! Everything contains the teachings of the true guru. From the spiritual perspective, all experiences are potential catalysts for inquiry.

You may feel as if you don't know what you're doing with regard to inquiry or ask yourself "Am I doing it?" That's okay. In fact, that's a good sign. If you already knew what you were attempting to look into, you wouldn't need to look into it. So it's natural to feel like you're fumbling about in the dark. A journey of discovery doesn't stick with what is known; it looks into what is unknown.

Pushing the Limits

In traditional martial arts, dedication to practice is fundamental for deeper understanding. Only through sustained, dedicated practice do we begin to understand what we had not previously imagined. The martial artist has to keep training through various doubts, plateaus, injuries, difficulties, and disillusionments. The spiritual journey is no different.

We have to trust there is a process at work, a path we're on. Our idea of where the path is going, however, and the reality of where it's going are not the same. So we have to pay attention. There are twists and turns. Sometimes we have to seek out other teachers, different methods, and new challenges. We have to be both determined and willing to plumb the depths of practice, go wherever the path leads, and transcend previous limits.

In a quest for the absolute, for the ultimate, it makes sense we would have to push ourselves to and beyond whatever limits we imagine. But when the absolute we're seeking is ever-present and always with us, what is the point of pushing? This is one of the many conundrums seekers find themselves in. We have to push, but no matter how much we push, pushing alone will not work.

The same is true of practice itself. You have to practice, but practice alone will not work. This seems like a paradox. Why practice so hard if the truth is ever present? But it's not as much of a paradox as it might seem. The path just doesn't actually work the way we usually think it does.

Simply put, we think we're striving toward the truth, but really we are striving to dispel delusions, to clarify, purify, and deconstruct what isn't true, what doesn't work, so that the truth can naturally shine through. That's all.

With this in mind, it makes sense our practice doesn't unfold how we imagine. There are many twists and turns because we are, ideally, discarding prior limitations and delusions along the way. That's why it's so important we push on, that we don't give up. It's a journey, and we discover where it leads only by actually going on the journey.

9

SEEKING EXPERIENCE

Q: You say experience is more important than theory, but at the same time you say enlightenment is not an experience. How do you reconcile this?

A: There is no need to reconcile anything. Some theory is good, and direct experience is essential. Look into everything, and let enlightenment take care of itself.

Unusual Internal States

Practitioners often explore, appreciate, and seek experiences of unusual internal states. These fall under a variety of names, such as trances, samadhis, one-pointed attention, visualizations, sensitivity, bliss, et cetera. Such states can provide insight, encouragement on the path, and some basic utility.

For a period in my twenties, I was meditating with white-hot intensity — straining the mind trying to find out what deep states were possible. Religious practice likewise led me into exalted states, such as during the Exsultet at midnight in a candle-lit cathedral, with clouds of incense hanging in air, when I wordlessly understood the essence of Christian teachings. Romantic love also took me into states of fervent devotion and manifest bliss. And throughout my martial-arts career, I was often trying to find and sustain elusive states of effortless action and reaction, or even a kind of extra-sensory perception.

For ambitious and earnest seekers plumbing the depths and limits of their consciousness and abilities, I don't think this is too unusual. Even for dabblers and curious participants just dipping their toes into practice, there's a sense of reaching for a different internal state for insight, understanding, and perhaps above all, relief.

Seeking and exploring states can be quite beneficial, particularly in the enthusiasm and clarification stages of our journey. The benefits are three-fold. One, delving into unusual states is a bit like flexing the mind, like a workout, expanding the mind's breadth and depth, preparing it for greater insight and understanding. Two, exploring unusual states can open the mind, provoke wonder and reveal how little we really know. Three, experiencing unusual states aids disillusionment through the failure of any state to bring lasting satisfaction. It's all throwing wood onto the fire.

Some traditions have mapped out successive states as stages or signposts on the way to enlightenment. In Patanjali's eight-limbs of yoga, for example, various meditative states correlate to a withdrawal of the senses, one-pointed focus, meditative absorption, and samadhi. There are then several kinds and levels of samadhi to be reached. Most fall into the category of temporary states and experiences. That's their limiting quality — they come to an end and one's normal life and world returns. Only final samadhis like *sahaja nirvikalpa samadhi* and *kaivalya* are unbroken and effortless ... and so fall outside the scope of practice or experience. They're more relevant to a discussion about enlightenment.

In the context of practice, letting go is the key to exploring states like samadhi, out-of-body experience, or religious exaltation. We can practice and push toward a particular or unfamiliar state, but when we feel ourselves at the threshold, we have to let go and *allow* it to happen. What are we letting go of? We are letting go of the known. What are we allowing to happen? We are allowing for the unknown. It's pure acceptance and emptying. If we continue to push at the threshold, or try to understand and know, we inevitably push away. So remember in your practice, when you feel yourself at a threshold, let go. It's a subtle movement of dropping off. It's not a thought or action — all that is known. It's just allowing whatever is happening to happen, without grasping, resistance, or judgment.

Siddhis and Powers

Some practices present the potential to develop what might seem like supernatural powers, or *siddhis.* Famous examples include levitation, bilocation, telepathy, clairvoyance, materialization, and so on. Because many people are curious about such powers, romanticize them, want to develop them, or believe enlightenment means gaining them or gaining them means enlightenment, it's an important discussion to have.

Try not to make assumptions or speculate about what various powers are, whether specific ones exist, and how they come about. There are, of course, people who can deceive others into thinking they have powers they don't have. In fact, that's a kind of power itself. But on a basic level, you know already that some people have powers you don't possess. For example, some people have an extraordinary sense of direction, or empathy, or the ability to make instantaneous calculations, or always seem to be at the right place at the right time. There are many levels of such powers, and they begin with things you can do already. Reading a book, for example, is a miraculous power!

In martial arts training, I had some experiences with people who had what seemed like almost supernatural powers. The ability to sense another's intentions, for example, countering attacks before they happen. The ability to remove the effects of punches, scramble the mind with a touch, and seemingly appear and disappear from an environment. Some of these powers I developed myself to some degree, at least enough to understand they weren't "magic."

Developing abilities we don't understand or previously seemed impossible is not a matter of "magic" or even necessarily spiritual development. But it does necessitate a change in perspective. It requires a kind of paradigm shift, seeing things that were not previously seen, and understanding things in a way that was not previously imagined. For example, one of my teachers used to tell me to *see* the fear and tension in others. At the beginning, seeing tension didn't make much sense, but eventually it was quite obvious. The first step was seeing, through experience, how much fear and tension I was carrying within myself. Just seeing that with some clarity changed the way I saw myself and others.

All too often, however, gaining power becomes an end unto itself. This is especially true in martial arts, where so many practitioners begin with fantasies about having power. But other practices and types of powers have within them the same trap. Such powers are of interest on the journey, and may serve to entice, motivate, confuse, open, correct, or encourage us on the path. But from a spiritual perspective, they are ultimately irrelevant.

Whatever powers we may attain, natural or supernatural, they are temporary and relate to the body-mind and world. Sometimes, arising spontaneously, they open the mind or point one onward. Sometimes they can be put to good use, such as healing or protecting others. But sometimes they are only a distraction. Pay attention if powers appear, but don't dwell on them, become attached them, or cling to ideas of developing or perfecting them.

If we become fixated on the idea we will gain powers through realization, we will surely put off realizing. True power comes only by surrendering to the higher power, by giving up all individual power. Someone asked me once if I could make an apple appear out of the air. "I am offering the truth," I said, "and all you want is more illusions. Go get an apple from the kitchen. There! You made it appear. I'm saying you have *already* made the entire universe appear, but you want apples."

True power comes not from developing or clinging to various limited powers, but by recognizing the higher power as one's true nature. Whatever appears and whatever happens is according to that higher power. Why concern yourself with what you can do or not do, with what happens or doesn't happen? Without changing a single thing, you are already all that ever was, is, or will be, right here and now.

At some point after my awakening, I discovered a type of levitation while meditating. The whole world disappeared, but my body remained in meditation posture, levitating in the vastness of the void. When I mentioned this to a student, he asked, "If you levitated like that, would I see it?" I laughed, "That's entirely up to you. But I can assure you, such levitation is possible." Alas, it's not something I practice because, while pleasant, it really isn't a big deal. I've come upon a few of these things out of curiosity and in order to understand and help others.

So yes, upon realization sometimes powers can arise. For one who has realized, however, such things are just a curiosity. It does not happen through effort or desire, and is no more astounding than a leaf, a rock, or anything else. Jnana itself is a treasure that transcends all powers and experiences. The Self alone is eternal and unchanging. Within it, all things appear — all subjects, all objects, and all powers. Just to know the Self is the greatest siddhi of all. So stay focused in your practice and don't become distracted by seemingly glamorous powers, abilities, or attainments.

Drug Experiences

Psychoactive substances have been used for millennia as part of spiritual practice. Ayahuasca, peyote, San Pedro, and various hallucinogenic mushrooms are well known for their use in traditional rituals and by a subset of spiritual seekers. Cannabis is used by sadhus and Rastafarians. LSD was championed by hippies and their college-campus descendants. While we might dismiss some of this as merely recreation, conscious and unconscious spiritual aspirations shouldn't be underestimated, now or in the past. The ancient Vedas speak of soma. The *Odyssey* speaks of Nepenthe. And numerous studies and ancient sources suggest that various types of drugs have long been associated with shamanic practices, spirituality, and spiritual paths.

Quite a few people who have contacted me with questions have had some experience with psychedelic drugs. Is this a coincidence? Do such experiences lead one to look deeper into a spiritual path? Or are people on a nascent spiritual path more likely to seek out these experiences for potential insight? Both are probably true, to some extent. Either way, it's a topic that should be openly discussed.

I generally advise against drug use, and certainly against regular drug use. I try to steer students directly toward the truth or, as needed, toward more stable practices. But considering the widespread use of drugs with some spiritual intention or context, it would be foolish to discount drugs entirely from a discourse on spiritual practice. Each person's journey is unique, and there *are* reasons these practices have appeared throughout time and across many different traditions.

Let's first establish that certain types of substances are commonly being used within a spiritual context. Setting aside mild stimulants like coffee or tea, we're talking about substances that can create highly-altered states of consciousness, significant distortions in perception, extraordinary experiences, heightened empathy, and insights into the nature of life, death, love, God, and reality. In other words, they sometimes induce a distinctly spiritual experience. Most of these drugs fall into the category of psychedelics and cannabinoids. There may be others, but those are the usual suspects.

What are the potential benefits? Perhaps the simplest answer is the potential to *open* the mind, to temporarily see things from a different view. The ordinary mind tends to fall into a particular view, a regular depth, focus, and pattern of thoughts, ideas, beliefs, perceptions, experiences, and interpretations. We take this view as reality. It may change over time, but it tends to change bit by bit, maintaining a continuity of cohesive delusion. As a result, the "reality" of the view rarely comes into question, and when it does, the questions are easily dismissed. The potential benefits of a drug experience come from its ability to break us out of the conditioned view, to see new things and familiar things, like oneself, one's thoughts, and one's life, from a wholly different perspective.

Some drug experimenters in the 60s believed the experiences they were having with LSD were more real or more spiritual than their everyday experience. That was a big mistake, and even they started to recognize the mistake with what they described as "the coming-down problem." Whatever exalted experience they had, it always passed. Of course! All states and experiences come and go. Under the influence of any drug, you will not experience anything fundamentally more real or more spiritual than your everyday life. The problem is not one of finding an exalted state. Reality itself is present in all states. The problem is that we don't recognize it — not in the everyday state, and not in the drug-induced state, either.

Remember, the truth of enlightenment is always present, so it cannot be anything new or transitory. From a spiritual perspective, the potential benefit of a drug experience is not from any special new thing or idea it reveals, but rather how contrast casts doubts on conditioned views. We move from one distortion to another, without ever really getting closer to the truth, but the sudden contrast between states naturally leads us to inquiry. That contrast can open the mind to questions about the self and reality, and encourage us to look deeper.

Of course, we may experience something extraordinary and, with the mind out of its rut, we could have insights that are helpful or healing in the context of our lives. That's no small matter, and with skilled guidance these experiences could have a powerful therapeutic effect. The underlying benefit, however, is the potential to ignite the fires of inquiry and lead us to question all views and experiences. In other words, the experience is just pointing out the way.

So what are the potential downsides, the risks and traps of this sort of practice? There are many and the stakes are high — no pun intended. A lack of studies, guidance, and regulation means numerous potential medical and social risks, including various types of addiction. Drugs often represent a kind of junk-food alternative to practices that require considerable time, effort, and discipline. Extreme experiences can lead to a so-called "bad trip." In other words, you could have a horrific experience, and/or the destabilizing effects could cause ongoing anxiety, paranoia, confusion, and fear. You could, essentially, experience something you're not ready for.

Because of the extraordinary nature of some drug experiences, another big risk is falling into the trap of chasing experiences or thinking the drug experience is somehow a kind of spiritual realization. In this case, the practitioner risks becoming a habitual drug user, ever chasing a bigger or better high or a more profound experience. They will end up just creating a new conditioned view, a new delusion, a new prison of the mind. And regular, habitual drug use ends up binding them to the very mind, body, and ego from which they might otherwise be liberated.

All this suggests while a limited experience with drugs could possibly have some benefit, it could just as easily be problematic, and habitual use, chasing experiences, or mistaking any experience for realization, are certainly traps. Extraordinary states are possible without any drugs whatsoever, and if you pay attention, there are already plenty of experiences that can open the mind. So drug use is one practice we can generally leave behind or avoid entirely. Whether people have had these experiences or not, benefited from them or not, I generally advise them to move on and take up a more stable practice. Or better yet, just recognize the truth now, in the ordinary, everyday waking state — no drugs required.

Wild Wisdom

Theia mania, divine madness, shamanic trances, left-hand paths, Zen antics, psychomagic, tricksters, and other forms of transgressive wisdom have existed across time, traditions, and cultures. Spiritual teachers who exhibit colorful eccentricities and transgress social norms are practically cliché. Unfortunately, sometimes genuinely abusive and criminal behavior is perpetrated under the name of spirituality. That kind of thing is best avoided, but there is a place for measured, skillful, transgressive wisdom both in teachings and practice.

Let's first note that a lot of respected spiritual teachers probably sounded a bit crazy to those who first heard them. Jesus is a great example here, for the Gospels chronicle how many people viewed his behavior as scandalous and his teachings as blasphemous. He hung out with prostitutes and tax collectors. He kicked over the tables of money changers. He said he came not for the righteous but for sinners. He said that he and God were one. At the time, this was all pretty scandalous stuff. And yet, there was God's wisdom in it.

Likewise, many accepted practices also can seem crazy to the uninitiated. When yoga meditation was introduced to the West, there were many who said it wasn't suitable to the "Western" mind, which was filled with too much activity. The undertones of racial superiority that often accompanied such assertions are deplorable, but the irony of thinking the mind is too active to meditate is hilarious. Yet the fact is, they saw sitting down and doing nothing as a somewhat crazy endeavor. Some people still think so, in the East and West alike. Alas, there are always some people who are too sick to take strong medicine. Other healing has to happen first.

On a very basic level, there's often an element of transgression in many spiritual teachings and practices, a sense of doing the opposite of what we might normally do. Teachings often turn expectations and norms on their head. Think about it. To be filled with thoughts, ideas, and activity is the norm. So practice by sitting down, clearing the mind, and doing nothing. To accumulate and hold on to money and possessions is the norm. So practice by giving money to the poor and letting go of possessions. To eat at regular intervals is the norm. So practice by fasting. The nature and function of practices are more complicated, of course, but an element of transgression is often there. It makes sense, since practices are meant to help clarify and transcend conditioned thoughts, habits, and views.

Perhaps the most sensational and extreme example of transgressive practices are those of India's Aghori sadhus. While many spiritual paths are moderately to extremely concerned with purification and avoiding defilement, the Aghoris welcome defilement and perform ritualized transgressions, going so far as to meditate on corpses, eat feces, garbage, and human flesh, smear their naked bodies with charnel-ground ashes, and have sex in the company of the dead. This is a left-hand path, which seeks to break social norms and find insight through profanity and transgression. It's not a path I recommend, but there is a rationale behind it — a way of breaking conditioned views and seeking God in even the lowliest and filthiest circumstances.

Drug experiences, as previously discussed, could also constitute a kind of transgressive wisdom. If I said, "Drink this potion. You will feel weird, probably throw-up, and may hallucinate, travel out of your body, and/or converse with spirit beings," it may sound a little crazy. It may even be a bit crazy, but nevertheless, it has helped some people on their path. Because sometimes something really far out is exactly what's needed to crack open the shell of an entrenched mind.

In my practice, I engaged in some fairly unusual martial-arts training. Practice involved giving and taking punches, being hit with sticks, whips, and chains, worked to the point of total exhaustion, kicked on the ground, thrown around like a rag-doll, twisted up like a pretzel, and enduring painful exercises and excruciating massages. It was usually done with compassion, skill, and the best intentions, but from a conventional view … a bit nuts. Such things are difficult to explain unless you experience them and learn the lessons they are meant to teach — how to stay calm under extreme stress, process pain and fear, heal injuries, remove negative thoughts, build relaxed strength, and see things clearly, inside and out. People who teach this kind of thing have to be very skillful, compassionate, and in control of their emotions and actions. But if done properly, these crazy practices can actually be a catalyst for direct inquiry and understanding oneself.

I have a friend who said his middle-school teacher told him he absolutely had to go outside at night, in the dark, without a light, and walk through a spider web. "It's amazing," the teacher said. "Absolutely wonderful!" Maybe it sounded a bit wild to the 8th-grade mind, but my friend had to try it, of course. One would be a fool not to! Although he didn't experience any kind of profound insight, he still remembers it to this day, which makes me wonder if he did have some insight that has reverberated through a lifetime of subsequent experiences and profound insights.

There's really no end to this kind of unconventional, wild wisdom. I'm not saying you should do every practice, act immorally, or obey any crazy thing a teacher tells you to do. That would be the opposite of wisdom. But when our goal is to transcend conditioned views, don't be afraid of unusual practices or some measured transgression as a way of storming the gates and finding insight along the way. Of course, walk away if you feel something is wrong, immoral, or abusive. Trust me, the paths to the truth are innumerable, and you have everything you need already. Because actually, life itself is filled with this wisdom. Everything we experience is filled with wild wisdom. All the twists and turns of our life, all the unexpected events, tragedies, mistakes, and adventures are really guiding us by virtue of a wisdom beyond our comprehension.

Experimentation

I would go so far as to say spiritual practice *must* have an element of experimentation. We cannot always be sure what we're doing. Even if we have a good teacher or follow in the path of an established tradition, we really have no idea what we're doing. How could we when we're seeking to discover the truth? So don't be afraid to experiment.

Regardless of the path we're on, what tradition we follow, and what instruction we've been given, we have to pay attention, ask questions, and discover for ourselves what works and doesn't work, what's real and isn't real, what's true and isn't true, about ourselves, the world, God, and reality itself. On that kind of journey, we have to be open to discovery and be willing to experiment. Exploration is vital because we learn through experience.

My own journey had many examples of experimentation. At sixteen, I found a book about yoga meditation and decided try it. At eighteen, I climbed Mt. Whitney in the dark after 25 days in the wilderness. At nineteen, a friend invited me to an Aikido class, and I said "Yes." At twenty, a guide invited me to spend the night in the tomb of a Muslim holy man in Central Java, and I said "Yes."

At twenty-one, I tried repeating paradoxical statements, meditating while staring into static on an old television, and recording myself describing what I saw while falling asleep. At twenty-eight, I learned to self-induce out-of-body experiences. At thirty-one, I was confirmed as a Catholic. At thirty-eight, I started training in Systema. At forty-two, a friend invited me to see his spiritual teacher, and I said "Yes."

These are just a few examples in a lifetime of seeking, experimenting, learning, and many times, just saying "Yes" when I didn't know where the path would lead. I'm not saying you have to do any specific things. Each person's journey is unique and will unfold accordingly. But we can look at this life and our spiritual journey as an adventure of discovery. Even if we never leave home and our only practice is meditation, we can still cultivate a sense of adventure and willingness to experiment, to look directly, to experience, and to see what's really there.

Remember, even the Buddha didn't know what he was doing when he set out on his spiritual path. He went to a succession of teachers who led him to deeper and deeper samadhis, but still he was not satisfied. He went into the forest with some like-minded seekers and practiced extreme asceticism, but after passing out from weakness, he saw this too would not work. Only after experimenting with so many possibilities and exhausting his hopes and ambitions did he finally find peace and liberation.

My own journey was a bit chaotic at times, so in some ways is a good example and in some ways a bad example. But the point I'm trying to make here is don't be afraid to try something. Don't be afraid to seek out a teacher, to try new practices or explore new states. Don't be afraid to ask questions, especially of yourself. Don't be afraid to look and see, to try and fail, to struggle and be disappointed or disillusioned. The path is self correcting. It's all part of the journey. Don't be afraid to go out in the middle of the night, in the pitch dark, and walk through a spider web. You may not realize the nature of reality then and there, but you will never regret doing it.

10

INTERNAL GUIDANCE

Q: Absent a teacher, what guides us on our spiritual path?

A: The true teacher is never absent. Your whole life is guiding you on the path. Just listen and pay attention.

Following the Code

In the classic detective novel, characters like Sam Spade and Phillip Marlow typically follow an ethical code, which guides their actions as good detectives. For example, they're tight lipped and keep a low profile. They protect the good from the bad. They break the rules if necessary when dealing with people who don't follow rules. They're loyal to clients, but more loyal to justice and the law. They keep an emotional distance and objectively examine the evidence at hand in order to solve cases.

Like this, many traditions have a defined ethical code, and following the code is a type of spiritual practice. The Abrahamic traditions have the ten commandments. The Buddhist tradition has the eight-fold path. They're both neatly encapsulated, but on some level, all traditions offer some kind of ethical code as guidance on being a good person, whether explicitly stated or not.

Many people consider such codes as a list of rules, a way of telling if you've been good or bad. But the code is more than just a list of *thou-shalts* or *thou-shalt-nots.* It articulates an underlying set of values that serve to aid a person on their spiritual journey. In the same way the detective's code functions with the goal of solving cases, the spiritual code functions to orient and guide practitioners toward the truth.

While following precepts may begin by adopting certain rules and making a commitment or taking a vow to follow them, something larger is going on with regard to this practice. Good precepts should lead one to selfless action and selfless action should lead one to selflessness itself. That's the idea, anyway.

We've been wandering in the wilderness and worshipping idols. From "Thou shalt have no other gods before me" all the way to "Thou shalt not covet," the commandments don't represent a mere rulebook. They represent a guidebook out of the wilderness we've been in. They represent a path back to God. Likewise, from "right view" all the way to "right samadhi," the eight-fold path represents a map pointing toward enlightenment.

Although the details, concepts, and language of such codes vary greatly from tradition to tradition, the general structure, purpose, and goal are the same. We can't understand the import of such codes unless we follow them — unless we actually walk the path. Only by putting forth effort in practice, struggling with our actions and our failures, and most importantly, struggling to understand ourselves, can we go where this path is meant to lead.

Interpreting Dreams

Dreams provide rich fodder for reflection. They are, however, seen through the sometimes disjointed, surreal, and cryptic symbology of the dreaming mind. Trying to make complete sense of dreams could just as likely lead you off track as on track. So what approach should we take with regard to dreams?

If you wish to incorporate dreams into your practice, the first step, of course, is to focus and pay attention. Many people say they don't dream or don't remember their dreams. There could be natural variation in dreaming or remembering dreams, but wherever you are on that spectrum, if you start to pay attention you will likely experience and remember more dreams. I suggest keeping a dream journal and having a way to record dreams quickly when you wake up.

As far as interpreting them … good luck! There are systems for interpreting dreams, but they're at best only primers on the kind of symbolism that *can* occur in dreams and not consistent symbolic references. Actual dreams can be quite perplexing. Like all sincere questions, constructed answers cannot represent the full picture.

Of course, many dreams may simply reflect processing of worldly events. Spend a day skiing and you might dream of skiing. Spend some time working in schools and you will have some dreams of dealing with students. Some studies suggest we're learning through such dreams — processing experiences and preparing for similar experiences.

Many straight-forward dreams can simply be noted. But sometimes you dream you're in a science station on an alien planet with a small team of astronauts. A black cat lives there too, and 1920's jazz plays on the intercom. The life support system starts going haywire, and everybody is struggling to fix it. Out a window you see a weird purple glow on the horizon, slowly getting closer, and suddenly know it's an alien intelligence. A witch shows up in one of the corridors and tries to tell you what to do. You run around frantically trying to fix things, but nothing seems to work. Eventually you, the other astronauts, and the cat abandon the station, taking off in a rocket. Before you break orbit, the rocket is enveloped in a purple cloud and the engines fail. Plummeting toward the planet, you know you will all die in moments. Nothing can stop it …

This dream isn't quite over, but you get the point: there's also this kind of dream. What could a dream like this mean? It's difficult to pull apart all the various elements and give them a meaning, and that would be somewhat foolish. It's more important to note the overall feeling of the dream. The isolation, the desperation, the sense of encountering an alien intelligence, the fear, and the impending doom are all significant. Note the overall feeling and trajectory of the dream, rather than trying too hard to assign specific meanings. Let the deeper meaning take care of itself.

There are certain types of dreams that speak directly to the difficulties we're facing on our spiritual journey. You might know when you've had one … or you might not. When I was a child, for example, I dreamt that I peeled away the skin on my hand, and beyond that thin layer of skin was nothing. At the time, it was sort of a weird, scary, somewhat disturbing dream. Now … that's quite interesting.

When you're chased by or encounter some kind of monster you can't quite get away from, can't quite directly face, and can't quite overcome … that's interesting. When you stand, float, or hover at the edge of an abyss … that's interesting. When a situation leads you toward an impending doom or if you actually die … that's very interesting. These are all relatively common dream scenarios that often speak directly to the spiritual journey.

So what should you do about it?

Nothing, really. For the most part, just note them, reflect on them and continue on your path. If in your dream you struggled to face a monster, or dive into an abyss, or fully die, for example, note this as a letting-go opportunity and set your intention to let go if the dream recurs. That's probably the most important thing. But don't get down on yourself if you can't do it in the dream. This kind of thing can go on for quite some time.

We have to allow dreams to work themselves out. That's true of waking life, too! We have to allow the process of our practice, whatever it is, dreaming or waking, to do its work on us. We do not *do* the process of practice. We simply engage with practice and the process does its work on us.

Lucid Dreaming

When you pay attention to your dreams, you may at some point become aware in a dream that you're dreaming. These lucid dreams allow for far-greater influence on the content and direction of a dream. Set your intention on waking within your dream and you may help this come about.

Why is this interesting? Aside from the novel experience and any entertainment you find in directing your dreams, lucid dreaming is yet another opportunity for spiritual practice.

Like many manipulating practices, we can get distracted and sidelined by merely entertaining or indulging ourselves. So it's not enough to just set the intention to wake up in your dream. You also have to make good use of the opportunity for practice.

Again, this is surprisingly similar to waking life. This remarkable life as a human being is an incredible opportunity for inquiry, practice, and realization. Yet too often we're distracted by an endless stream of selfish and egoic desires. In fact, the distractions we pursue in lucid dreams are likely the same distractions we pursue in waking life.

So if you do happen to realize you're dreaming while dreaming, try to make the most of it, especially if you're in a dream that may already be spiritual in nature. If you find yourself standing at the edge of an abyss, dive in! If you encounter a monster, face it without fear. If you die, don't look back — go fully into death and see what happens. Whatever is happening, you can also just sit down and continue your meditation practice.

What can go wrong? It's only a dream.

Healing the Body and Mind

The trajectory of our lives imprints into our bodies and minds many injuries, imbalances, pains, anxieties, fears, neurotic thoughts, and negative emotions. Traumas, great and small, stay with us, and after a few decades, just dealing with ourselves can feel like a significant strain or even an overwhelming burden.

Somehow, we keep making the same mistakes and inflicting the same kinds of wounds on ourselves … or deepening our existing wounds. When will we stop? How will we stop? Can we ever heal ourselves?

Sorting this out, reversing this trend, and healing ourselves of these afflictions can be an integral part of spiritual practice. Whether through introspection, meditation, yoga, prayer, and so on, healing the body and mind, removing imbalances and chronic tensions can serve as a spiritual guide.

Suffering must be known and the cause of suffering also known. We must be willing to look at our pain and its causes. What are the causes within ourselves? Many people have trauma related to some kind of abuse, and I'm not dismissing the role of others in anybody's pain. But like it or not, we're also involved, and to begin healing we have to start with ourselves.

In all our practices, whatever they are and whichever direction they go, we will still have to deal with ourselves. So however we go about it, getting to know ourselves and our suffering, and inquiring into their cause and nature, are an important part of the journey, regardless of path, practice, or mode. Real healing is a process of undoing the tangles of delusion — of our desires and our aversions.

Pay attention to the body and mind. Note how they operate, how thoughts arise, how emotions bloom, how fear spreads, how ideas perpetuate themselves, how injuries happen, how pain is magnified, and so on.

We will only stop adding to our troubles when we're willing to start regarding ourselves with kindness. We only find healing by letting go of the attachments that support and reinforce our pain and suffering. We cannot do it by fixing everything — it's simply not possible. Along the way, we may fix a few things, but we will only find real relief by letting go of the self that holds on to all this pain and suffering.

Working with Emotions

The course of life takes us on a roller coaster of positive and negative emotions. Sometimes it feels like a gently undulating kiddie coaster. Other times it feels like a demon coaster, complete with death drops, loops, spirals, and dark tunnels.

For the most part, we ride the coaster and just hang on. We enjoy the view at the peaks, and we lose our stomachs in the troughs. When inverted we hope we don't fall out, and in the darkness we wait for the light. The experience as a whole can be exhilarating, but this metaphor only goes so far.

In our lives and practice, we often cling to the ups and resist the downs. Because of this, we can work with these ups and downs as part of our spiritual practice. They become, in a way, the object of the meditation that is the whole of our lives.

It's not just a matter of managing or even mastering our emotions. Of course, some basic managing is necessary and helpful when we're feeling overloaded. Self-acceptance, self-compassion, and self-kindness should be practiced, especially if we're struggling with traumatic experiences or powerful emotions. A little bit at a time, layer by layer if needed, we have to face ourselves with acceptance and compassion.

Ultimately we should practice cultivating equanimity, and not cling to the ups or resist the downs. Observe the cyclical nature of the emotional ups and downs in your days, weeks, months, years. When you notice all emotional states are temporary — they all pass — it's easier to be okay with the downs and let go of the ups, without clinging, disappointment, frustration, or despair. It's okay to be sad, and it's okay to let go when good things come to an end.

A wise friend once told me that suffering comes from rejecting reality, and that's exactly right. When you're sad, you are *already* sad. Accept this sadness — be okay with it — and it will transform, if not instantaneously, then over time, as sure as day dawns after a long night. When good things pass, they are *already* passing, like day into night. Rest assured this is the natural order of things.

A wonderful thing happens when we practice this kind of acceptance and equanimity. The jarring aspects of the roller coaster are smoothed out, and the whole ride — the ups and the downs — become easier and more enjoyable. The fact is, we enjoy the ups more when we don't cling to them or try to amplify them. And we can even, in a way we hadn't imagined before, "enjoy" the downs as well.

Cultivating equanimity brings us closer to reality. Working with our emotions frees us from their jarring effects and allows for consistent kindness, far-reaching compassion, and immense joy.

11

MAKING PROGRESS

Q: How do we know we are making progress on the path?

A: Put forth effort in practice until effortlessness is realized. Then you will dissolve into reality. There will be nothing left.

System vs No System

You might wonder if you should follow a particular tradition and singular course of practice. Is that better than skipping around? Are you likely to make more progress? Is one system or practice more direct than another?

There is no single answer. The right path really depends on the whole situation.

Remember the Buddha himself was not a Buddhist, and his path led him to a number of different teachers and practices. Only after mastering everything those teachers had to offer and trying all those practices without satisfaction did he resolve to sit under a tree until enlightenment. If he had sat there at the beginning, would he have awakened?

We can only speculate on an answer, but it shows how the path, when taken as a whole, can be quite circuitous, even for a Buddha. The ego-self is a tangled bundle of sticky thoughts. It's a Gordian knot! Who knows what we might have to do or go through in order to untangle it. And so, we have to be willing to go where the path leads.

There are two competing aspects to practice. On the one hand, we have to commit. We have to practice consistently and go deeply. We cannot give up after our initial enthusiasm wanes or when difficulties arise. We cannot flounder when we fall into confusion or plateau in our efforts at clarification. We cannot be discouraged when we get a taste of disillusionment. We have to keep going. We have to be dogged in our determination. On the other hand, we have to really listen and go where our practice leads. Sometimes it leads us to a different practice. It might say, you need to do this other thing for a while or take a step back to work this out. If we don't listen and go where our practice leads, we'll get stuck in our current stage.

We can use martial arts as an example. Even if you don't do martial arts, you can probably relate. If you don't commit to training consistently with determination within a particular art, you will just flounder about and not improve your skill or understanding with any depth. Only by transcending the imaginary levels and limitations can we deepen understanding. At the same time, however, some perceived lack, limitation, or deficit can necessitate a new teacher, new practice, or new art. It's better to adapt and change than to be stuck.

I practiced Aikido for over twenty-five years, but I still felt something was missing, some measure of confidence or martial efficacy. In reality, I had not faced and dealt with my fear. So I sought out another teacher and trained in Systema, which helped push me beyond that sticking point. It's not that I abandoned Aikido. On the contrary, I went exactly where Aikido had led me. That was necessary to move beyond and realize what my practice was trying to show me.

So, what's needed is not necessarily this or that particular practice or tradition but, rather, dogged determination combined with the sensitivity and willingness to go where directed. With these qualities, the path is self-correcting. We can just focus on doing the work, wherever it leads.

Consistency is Magic

With regard to progress, I cannot stress enough the importance of consistency. Repetition and consistent practice ushers us toward transformation. We cannot transform ourselves. Our part is to put forth effort and engage in practice — to let go of ourselves and to allow the deeper process to do its work.

What does this mean in practical terms? It means, for example, ten minutes of meditation every day is better than an hour every six days. It means regularity is more important than intensity. It means dedication is more important than natural aptitude.

Of course, some natural aptitude is good, and it's important to push ourselves with intensity once in a while. But the real transformative magic happens through consistent application of practice.

Don't count on the force of your will alone. Don't rely on inspiration. It's not enough to just hear the teachings. We have to actually commit to consistent practice.

Make practice a habitual part of your daily life. At the beginning, practicing may seem like a struggle, so make it as convenient as possible. For example, if you want to develop a meditation practice, leave the cushion out and sit on it every day. Once you have the habit, you will naturally start to sit longer and go deeper.

Sometimes you will feel like you aren't making any progress at all. That's okay. Not everything that's happening will be immediately apparent to you. The effects of our practice often remain below our conscious awareness for a long time. But one day you will notice you're not the person you were ... or that you're not a person at all.

Life Stages

Depending on how old you are, you may have noticed your life seems to pass through various stages. When we consider our memories, we tend to categorize life stages based on situations and circumstances, and we can divide and subdivide them in various ways. Contemplating these stages may give you some insight into where you are now, and where you may be heading.

In the Hindu tradition, there's a well-thought-out system of dividing life into four stages, or *ashramas*. The first stage is *Brahmacharya,* characterized by abstinence and education. The second stage is *Grihasta,* meaning "householder," and is dedicated to marriage, sex, family, business, wealth, et cetera. The third stage is *Vanaprastha,* meaning "forest dweller," and represents retirement, passing on the responsibilities of the household to the next generation, and withdrawing to a life more dedicated to spiritual concerns. The fourth stage, entered at any point, is *Sannyasa,* which is wholly dedicated to renunciation, asceticism, and the spiritual path.

This gives a nice backdrop of some broad categories that, in many regards, hold up across cultures. Many of us think of our life's stages with a bit more specificity, such as infancy barely remembered, early childhood, school, first love, that time I worked at the bank, that time I dated so-and-so, marriage, parenting, getting interested in or practicing this or that, and so on. However you break it up, there's always a sense of various situations forming, building up, progressing, and then dissipating, breaking apart, and falling away.

The stages of life are always like that. In other words, they're like all things — each stage comes and goes in its own way and its own time. The various situations arise and entangle to form a larger, more complex situation that is later remembered as a stage. The situations change and develop until they disentangle, fall apart, and give rise to the next stage. This is the natural way of things and life stages. There is nothing to fear in the coming and going of various stages.

The whole of life is like that, too. It comes into being through the confluence and entanglement of various elements and situations. It changes and develops until it eventually disentangles and falls apart. Again, this is the natural way of things, and is nothing to fear. On the contrary, it's quite wondrous. It's life's great adventure!

We spend the first part of our lives forming and building up various elements. This is what childhood is about, what being a student is about, and what being a householder is about. It's all a matter of increasing entanglements, responsibilities, and the consequences and results of those elements, situations, and actions. Along the way, the identity becomes more and more solidified as that tangle itself. In the second part of life, we have the possibility and the opportunity to direct our efforts toward disentangling from whatever mess we've gotten ourselves into. It's a process of letting go. We can say, "I'm going to go off into the forest now to contemplate the meaning of life, the universe, and everything." We can say, "I'm going to go back to being nobody."

Keys to Progress

Like life, spiritual practice progresses through stages, according to circumstances, effort, and the overall causal forces (karma) at work in our lives. Ultimately, these stages are not separate, but in the midst of practice we can consider progress as a series of stages.

Anybody who has engaged in practice long enough will know there are ebbs and flows in motivation and attention, determination and skill, insight and understanding. When we're new to practice, these changes may trouble or discourage us, but seasoned practitioners know this ebb and flow is part of the journey.

We've already characterized the stages of the journey, but let's review them and look at each stage more closely to understand the keys to progress.

Contact

With Contact, we encounter and become interested in life, experience, phenomena, and teachings. This has nothing to do with practice and comes about on its own, due to causal forces. But contact leads to wonder and some initial question, like "What the heck is going on?" or "What is the meaning of life?" *Interest* in searching for an answer sets us off upon our journey.

Enthusiasm

With Enthusiasm, we get excited about possible answers, particular teachings, or practices that sound promising. We may start a practice, but if our enthusiasm wanes or the practice gets boring, we just move on, looking for another teaching or practice that excites us. The key to progress here is *motivation*. When sufficiently motivated, we commit to regular practice without relying on the caprice of enthusiasm.

Commitment

In Commitment, we go through some kind of initiation, formal and/or symbolic, and commit to serious practice. We build the habits and attributes necessary for the journey ahead. We practice consistently through the ups and downs to develop focus, sensitivity, and awareness. The key to progress here is not to become complacent with just going through the motions of consistent practice. We need *dedication* to plumb the depths of practice with a will to the truth. Then we will naturally begin our struggle for clarification.

Clarification

In Clarification, we really get into the thick of practice, and for many people this is the bulk of the journey. Here we struggle with numerous difficulties, the paradoxes of teachings, the subtleties of spiritual traps, along with our confusion, doubts, troubles, insights, views, and experiences — good, bad, and indifferent. We practice in order to purify our ego, heal our body-mind, and transcend various obstacles, obstructions, and defilements. The key to progress is the *courage* to seek truth above all and a willingness to let go of false views. When we have seen through enough traps and obstacles, we will start to become disillusioned with all conditioned and constructed views.

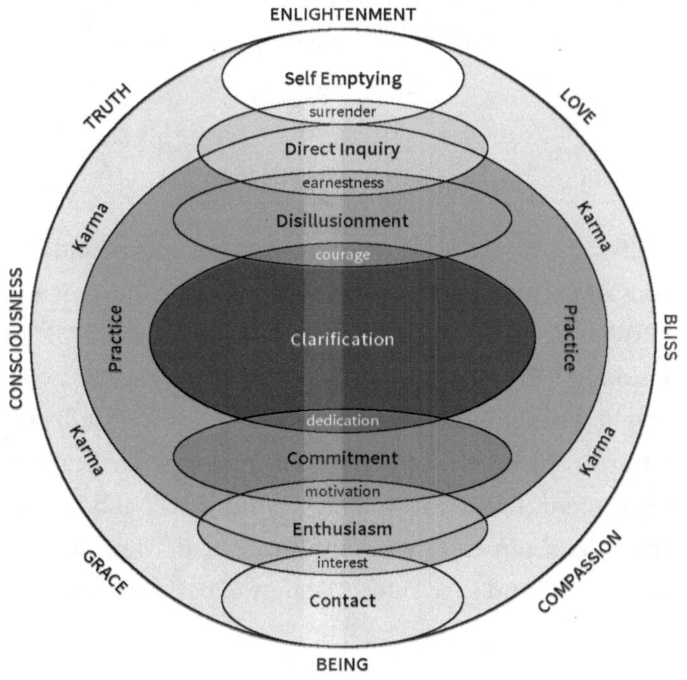

Disillusionment

In Disillusionment, all views are regarded as inadequate, false, and unsatisfying. We can no longer play the game of beliefs and views. We can no longer make decisions based on views. We have no real opinions to offer, and not much to say about anything. We are tired of Samsara, but we go on, because there's nothing else to do. If disillusionment is not complete, it will taste bitter, and we may turn away and go back for more Clarification. Although dissatisfied with views, we are still bound by them, so the experience of disillusionment can be troubling — a dark night of the soul. Continued practice is helpful to ward off despair, and essential for taking practice beyond particular views. The key to progress is *earnestness,* the sincerity and conviction to follow where the path leads.

Direct Inquiry

In Direct Inquiry, we look directly into the most fundamental mysteries of existence - the very cornerstones of our view. *Who am I? What is God? What is time? What is space? What is consciousness?* Direct Inquiry goes beyond thoughts and views to seek insight through present experience. However, it's still possible to fall into traps here, circling back for more Clarification and Disillusionment. Endeavor to look to your direct and immediate experience, and not to rely on any thought or view. The key to progress is profound surrender. We may experience deep insight, but the fruit of Direct Inquiry is not a new view; it is the falling away of all views.

Self-Emptying

In the Self Emptying stage, everything falls away: all views, all beliefs, life, death, self, mind, body, and world. There is nothing to be done here, nobody to do it, and no progress to be made. We are cast adrift, unmoored from what we had previously taken to be reality, which now appears dreamlike. The veil of separation has fallen — self and world appear seamlessly — but we have not yet realized oneness. The spontaneous awakening of Enlightenment has not yet occurred.

Enlightenment

Enlightenment is not really a stage at all. Knowledge of the One is outside time and space, outside causation and progress. It is without separation or duality. What more can be said? See the previous books for more in-depth discussions on the topic of Enlightenment.

We're using these stages as an orientation to where we are and where we're going, but it's only a map. Our journey is unique. We have to follow our actual path and not just rely on a map. The map makes progress look linear, but actually we progress in bits and pieces, in loops and spirals. We can go backward. We can be in different stages in different areas of our lives. We can skip steps or pass through them so quickly we don't even notice. We can go through wormholes, forward, backward, or sideways. We can catch glimpses of other states and stages. None of this can be represented on a simple map of stages.

Contrary to the way many people think about progress, it's not a matter of reaching for something new, a new state or stage. It's more a matter of doing the work at hand, and letting go of previous views, states, and stages. If we just keep going with determination and resolve, through all the struggles and plateaus, progress happens on its own.

See your struggles, plateaus, and frustrations as nothing other than signs of progress. There is a process at work. You know very little, if anything, about it. But you have to trust the process is at work and has the power to transform you.

At least through the stages that involve practice, your part is just to put in the effort and continuously let go. Commitment, effort, and determination matter greatly through the middle stages. Beyond Clarification, there is less and less for us to do, until we can do nothing at all. Ultimately, from beginning to end, everything happens according to a higher power.

12

FINAL APPROACH

Q: I have been practicing for a long time, and often feel I am close to the truth, but for some final barrier I cannot seem to cross.

A: Leave yourself behind, and you will have no trouble.

Renunciation

Like asceticism, when we think of renunciation we tend to think of the extremes of religious practice. Those who renounce worldly life and live in caves, cells, or cloisters are certainly renunciants in the general sense of the term. But a deeper sense of renunciation is at the heart of all spiritual practice.

What does renunciation really mean? It's not what we consider the typical outward signs — for example, giving up money, pleasure, comforts, and social or familial activities or contacts. Although those signs may occur or be taken on as practice, they are not the essence of renunciation, which is simply turning away from delusion. The inward renunciation is what's important, not the outward signs, which can take different forms.

For so long we've pursued our desires, our ideas, our beliefs, our concepts, and our goals. For so long we've put the ego and its entanglements at the center of awareness. And for so long we've suffered on the wheel of effects these egocentric views produce.

The spirit of renunciation is a feeling of being tired of all that. We've been on the wheel for some time. We've gone around the cycles of our life enough to know what it has to offer, and to know that egoic consciousness is not ultimately satisfying. We may have experienced moments of relative happiness, but they're too soon gone, and more like brief respites from suffering than true happiness. And we know, deep down, all future prospects are like that.

We can aspire to and practice renunciation. But true renunciation comes as a gift, an immense blessing that no ego-self could bring about. For true renunciation means turning away from the ego-self, from our selfish and deluded views, and in fact from all views.

True renunciation is total disillusionment and has the power to transform our lives. No longer are we pursuing our desires, our ideas, our beliefs, our concepts, and our goals. No longer are we living a life rooted in the ego-self. Renouncing all that, we live a life rooted in emptiness — but an emptiness from which kindness, compassion, joy and equanimity flow without limit or end.

Folding Everything In

Many people on the spiritual path struggle to formulate a full intellectual understanding of what truth and realization mean or what total perception entails. Many struggle with understanding what the mind is or what the self is. Many struggle with various hang-ups, from feelings of inadequacy to endless tasks that must be completed. For all these struggles, I prescribe the practice of *folding everything in.*

Let's start with this: The truth isn't complicated; it just doesn't leave anything out. In other words, nothing can be outside of everything. So whatever you think your hang-up is, it's not separate from the truth you seek. In fact, it's the very door to awakening. If only we can fold everything in and see that nothing is separate, nothing stands apart, then we see there are no hang-ups, struggles, or conflicts that can bar us from the truth.

Generally, as we try to think through things, we're always keeping something separate. We always keep ourselves ignorant of some things in order to analyze other things. For example, when examining objects or the world, we keep ourselves separate. When examining ourselves, we keep the world and others separate. When thinking about life, we leave out death. When thinking about death, we leave out life.

This mental habit of separating and isolating is the work of maya, which keeps us unaware of Unity. Maya can be very tricky, because it also keeps us largely unaware of *what* we're leaving out.

So the practice is to watch for what you're leaving out, and to fold that into everything.

For example, some people will catch an intellectual glimpse of emptiness and fall into a nihilistic or negative view. The problem here is they haven't been thorough. While jumping to the conclusion the world isn't real or has no meaning, they keep themselves out of the mix. They retain reality and meaning for the ego-self, and so fall into nihilism. If they could fold themselves, and whatever else they're holding back, into emptiness, a very different experience would emerge.

In the months prior to my awakening, I wrestled with the question, "What is my mind and where did it come from?" I thought my mind was something separate from other things. The breakthrough came while I was driving home from work one day, along a winding mountain road lined with Douglas firs and dark, mossy forests. Seeing the world and everything that had grown out of it, I realized my body and mind had also grown out of that. My mind was no different than the trees! Everything was the same, inside and outside, mind, body, and world.

This folding-in experience is what I have described as a culminating thought, or final thought. It's a thought that at last folds everything into one — even the mind and the thought are folded in. When nothing is left out, consciousness is prepared for awakening.

The End of Practice

Practice is essential for clarifying the mind, body, and world. It is necessary for determining what is real and unreal, what is transient and eternal. And the earnestness, effort, and determination we put into practice are integral to the process.

The journey may be short and direct or long and circuitous, but if we follow our practice all the way to the end, one way or another it brings us to the doorstep of awakening. There, everything begins to fall away, even practice. To be clear, one may go on practicing — out of habit, enjoyment, dedication, or service — but one is no longer practicing for oneself. The wheel is still turning, but the engine has stopped.

So if you come to a point where your practice seems empty, where it seems pointless or futile, you can just keep going. There's nothing to be concerned about. If you need a reason for practice, dedicate your practice to the benefit of others. But as for yourself, move toward emptiness, become more and more comfortable with it, with being nobody, with wanting nothing, with seeking nothing.

When mind, body, self, and world are emptied out — nothing left apart, everything folded into emptiness — consciousness is at the threshold of enlightenment.

Here, no practice can help you. Fundamentally, although you may not have realized it yet, there is no self to help. Put forth no effort. Just let go of whatever thoughts remain.

Post-Enlightenment Practice

While we're on the subject, we should say something about practice after enlightenment, in case any readers find themselves in this situation. In some ways, nothing changes. If practice continues, it just continues, that's all. But in some ways, everything changes, and this post-enlightenment practice is an entirely different topic than the practice we've been discussing.

Before realization, we were practicing with something in mind. After realization, if we practice, we do so with no mind. Before, we were seeking; afterward, there is nothing to seek. Before, we were hoping for results; afterward, our greatest hopes are here already. Before, we were full of desires, be it for answers, recognition, bliss, or security; afterward, we abide in peace.

After my awakening, I sat down to meditate as I had before, and after a few minutes, I thought, *This is weird.* The more I *tried* to meditate, starting with some measure of effort, desire, motivation, and direction, I felt myself moving away from the truth, not deeper into it. In fact, I was *already* in a deep meditative state and the mind was already clear. No effort was needed.

In some way, practice itself assumes separation. Finding our way out of separation is the whole point of practice. Once one has found peace, what practice is needed? Once one has found truth itself, what inquiry could be fruitful?

So one has to change one's whole approach to practice. First, the purpose of practice is different. Simple curiosity, enjoyment, or to instruct and help others are the primary reasons for practice now. Second, the way one goes about practicing is also different. It is effortless, without striving, and without personal goals or direction.

Truly, the enlightened one's practice is just to abide in peace, and reflect the truth one has realized with generosity and fearlessness — through kindness, joy, compassion, and equanimity.

PART FOUR

DEALING WITH DIFFICULTIES

Wherein we offer targeted advice regarding some common difficulties in practice.

13

OVERARCHING CONDITIONS

Q: Wouldn't the path be easier if I became a monk?

A: No, it would be just as difficult. The circumstances have nothing to do with it. You don't have to become a monk to understand your difficulties and address them.

General Difficulties

Spiritual practice is not without difficulties. Nobody said practice was easy, and in fact, the difficulties are essential. The difficulties themselves give us something to transcend. Grasping itself, for example, gives us something to let go of. Confusion itself gives us something to clarify.

Previously, we identified the main traps in each of the four paths as conceptualism, idolatry, hypocrisy, and egotism. We showed how each trap results from the same basic "mistake," taking things to be real that are not fundamentally real. And we discussed how the crux of this problem is always oneself, the first thing we take to be real in this way. All other obstacles rely on this one, so transcending the individual self is the main prerequisite for realization.

That's where we're heading, but for practitioners deep in the woods of practice, there can be more pressing matters that require immediate attention. So let's explore practical advice for some of the more common difficulties we may encounter on the path.

It's all well and good to transcend, but if you're tied to a tree, deep in a demon-haunted forest with night approaching, you may need more targeted advice. If you encounter a tiger walking along a path, you may need instructions on how to survive. If you're weary from travel and just want to lie down and drift off into dreams, you may need encouragement. If you're lost in nihilism, you may need help to find the way out.

These difficulties can be quite specific to the situation and the individual, and the best advice should take that into account. Nevertheless, we can endeavor to offer advice for some common difficulties, without losing sight of the fundamental difficulty at the heart of the matter.

Endless Tasks & Perfect Conditions

When it comes to engaging in serious practice, there's always something at hand to help us procrastinate. We think, *I'll really get down to it once I have a few things sorted out.* We think, *Once this situation has passed, or once conditions are better, then I'll get serious.* But there's a flaw with these ideas.

Wanting to complete other tasks first becomes just an excuse to put off practice. We think practice will be easier once we have the attic cleaned out and all the old photographs sorted, once we finish our obligations to the book club, once the kids are out of the house, or once the divorce is settled. Or, at the extreme, we think, *If only I could retreat to a cave in the mountains, then I could really practice!*

However this difficulty appears, in the subtle form of endless little tasks or in the extreme form of wanting a complete retreat from our current situation — wanting perfect conditions — there are two mistakes we're making.

First, there is no end to these kinds of things. Life has a way of continually creating new tasks and obligations, new unfinished business. Just accept there will always be unfinished business, right up until the moment you die. That's how things are. Sure, maybe you can settle a few big pending things, but if you think you will ever wrap everything up neatly, either in your mind or in the world, you will always be frustrated. Even if you retreat to a cave, you will still have unfinished business in your mind — and you will still have to deal with it.

Second, sincere practice will always be challenging. It will be no less challenging after you've completed a thousand tasks or after you've moved to a cave or monastery. However many things you complete or set right, the mind can always find more. The difficulty lies not in setting ten-thousand things right, but in setting your mind right. So best get to practicing here and now. There is no better situation and no other time.

You may detect, even in this moment, numerous objections and exceptions. I can hear the thoughts of many readers. *What about this? What about that? Surely it makes sense to take care of this first?* — No! There is no other time. Putting off your practice will not help in any way whatsoever, but practicing will help in innumerable, unfathomable ways.

Sustaining Effort

The greatest impact we can have on the course of our path is through earnest effort put forth in practice. Until effortlessness is realized, effort is unavoidable, so we are well advised to direct that effort toward our highest aspirations. A common difficulty is just sustaining effort through all the ups and downs. How can we maintain effort over the long term?

First, we should do whatever we can do to articulate and remind ourselves of our intentions and aspirations. Setting these intentions in the mind helps the subconscious keep working, even when our willful effort lags behind. That's why monks take vows and wear robes, as signs of intention and aspiration. That's why various traditions have prayers to punctuate the day, as reminders of our highest destiny.

If you're not a monk or a follower of any particular religion or spiritual tradition, you should find ways to create these little reminders in your life and practice. Small rituals, token objects, habitual prayers, can all serve as reminders of your intentions and aspirations. They can be as subtle or as visible as you like. Just remember, the purpose is not to remind others, but to remind yourself.

Second, endeavor to make practice a regular and integral part of your day. If your practice is always something separate from your life, tagged on, or interjected at irregular intervals, it will be much more difficult to sustain. Sheer force of habit and a practice integrated into your daily rhythms will help you persevere when effort is lagging.

Again, for a monk or religious devotee, regularity is built into the monastic or religious life. For a secular person, that regularity must be created and integrated into life's daily rhythms. Consider this deeply, because these structures can really help keep us practicing. Structure allows us to apply what effort we have where it's needed most and not waste it just trying to get to the starting line.

Third, acknowledge that it's natural for effort to ebb and flow according to the situations of our life and the course of our practice. Avoid judging yourself when effort is low. There may be good reasons, and such judgment is generally not helpful. If you notice effort is low, just gently return your attention to practice and press ahead without grasping or resistance. That's all.

Insufficient Energy

On the Buddha's quest for enlightenment, he learned many practices. Eventually he went into a forest to practice extreme asceticism, sleeping outside, wearing only a loincloth, eating little or nothing. After a long time without success, one day he fainted from weakness. It seemed likely he would die of starvation before realizing the truth, so he accepted some food and started eating again.

Engaging in spiritual practice takes effort and energy. Without adequate energy, sooner or later our practice falters. If body and mind are overloaded, we risk spending all our effort just tending to various troubles. If we don't take care of ourselves and lose all balance in our lives, we'll be hard pressed to find the energy needed for dedicated spiritual practice.

The Buddha taught a middle way between rigid asceticism and sensual over-indulgence, both of which can tax the body and mind, leaving us fatigued and languishing. Both extremes trap us in unhealthy and unsustainable activity. Both trap us in a cycle of identification and dependent behaviors, rather than leading to fruitful practice and liberation.

If we don't eat, we become weak, fatigued, and prone to various ailments. If we overeat, we also become weak, fatigued, and prone to various ailments. Likewise, if we don't sleep enough, we become overly tired. If we sleep too much, we also become overly tired. If we work all the time to take care of the ego, we become bound to ego-involvement. If all we do is entertain the ego, we also become bound to ego-involvement. The same is true for all the areas of our lives. Any extreme unbalances the body-mind and leads to lack of energy.

Many people are living lives wildly out of balance in one way or another. We eat unhealthy foods, don't sleep enough, watch too much television, scroll too much media, work too much, worry too much, and so on. We're all acquainted with these modern issues, yet we often compensate for doing too much by doing even more.

Most will ignore spiritual practice because they just don't have the time or energy. Some will pile on spiritual practice as one more busy task to check off or one more activity to consume or get through. A few will become fanatically obsessed with improving their behavior or perfecting their lifestyle. All these reactions are problematic in the long run. So much more benefit could be had by just toning things down and not falling into any extremes.

Of course, there are times when our practice requires hard training and concentrated effort. Sometimes even extreme practices are necessary along the way. But over a lifetime of practice and service to others, balance facilitates our greatest potential. Make small changes to cultivate habits conducive to balance, and your practice will flourish, like a seed planted in fertile soil.

Lacking Discipline

Some people lament that while their intentions are there and their aspirations are high, they seem to lack the discipline required for regular spiritual practice. Everything we said regarding sustaining effort and energy applies here as well, but to address discipline, let's talk about the importance of building habits rather than relying on some notion of personal will power.

If you think discipline is a matter of will power, you will be disappointed time and time again. Sure, an iron will might help a little at the beginning, but will power is not the driving force of discipline. If that's all you're relying on, discipline will fail sooner or later. It might be better to forget about will power altogether. Imagine you have no will power, and just focus on building habits that will further your practice.

Considering habits as the driving force of discipline allows you to proactively develop discipline, rather than relying on some imagined innate quality like will power or discipline itself. Just focus on identifying and building habits conducive to practice.

With this frame of mind, we can look into how habits are formed and what contributes to building them easily and effectively. Although this can apply to any practice, let's use meditation as an example. Imagine you aspire to meditate daily, but it never seems to work out, or you're constantly struggling to make it happen. What can you do to build this habit? Here's my advice: set a regular time, make it easy, and increase in small increments. Let's go through them one by one.

Regular Time

Set aside a window of time in your daily schedule for your core meditation. Create at least a half-hour window, even if you only intend to meditate for ten minutes. Make it a daily or twice-daily occurrence. Regularity over time will help build a solid habit.

Make it Easy

Make it easy on yourself by setting aside a space for your practice, putting out the cushion, and leaving everything out and ready to go. Make this space in an area you frequent, not in the basement or the attic. The easier you make it to do the practice, the less resistance you will have to doing it.

Small Increments

Start with just a short meditation at the prescribed time. Even just five minutes is good, if building the habit from nothing. Increase the time in five-minute increments when you feel ready. By starting modestly and not ramping up too quickly, you acclimate to practice and increase the chance of sticking with it.

Once you have a regular practice built on habit, you can start pushing and exploring deeper practice. And you've done it all without having to rely too much on will power or some notion of innate discipline.

14

CAUGHT IN LIFE

Q: Just when I seem to be making progress in my practice, my life and ego has a way of roaring back in with a vengeance. How can I stop this from happening?

A: Your life is your practice. Don't see the antics of your ego as an obstacle, but rather a phenomenon to be investigated. When you understand what the ego really is and what you really are, these problems will vanish.

Confusion

Confusion is to be expected within your practice. After all, clarifying this confusion is the whole reason for our spiritual journey. If everything was perfectly clear, there would be no need to clarify anything. But if confusion becomes too troubling, leads to obstacles, or flagging practice, some advice and encouragement may be needed.

For example, if you find yourself confused and struggling to make sense of a book, just relax and keep reading. If necessary, approach the text as a kind of enigmatic poem. Trust that merely by reading, even without immediate understanding, the seeds of clarification are being planted. In other words, there's a process at work, and understanding begins below our immediate awareness.

The same is true for our meditation, mantras, prayers, inquiry, and so on. Try not to be surprised or discouraged if you encounter some confusion. It's a sign you're putting forth sincere effort on the path. Unless you've already fully awakened to the truth, I would be more concerned if you *weren't* at least a little confused.

With confusion, we can be tempted to prematurely give up on practice and our search for the truth. That's something I went through. While sometimes this is necessary or unavoidable, leading us from practice to practice until all the various seeds begin to take root, eventually we have to persevere through this confusion.

In order to persevere, we need to have some trust in the process of practice. Even though we may be confused and don't entirely understand what we're doing, where it's going, and the effect it's having, we trust the process and continue with practice. That's the only way to see where consistent practice leads.

This is where an association with a well-established tradition or a good teacher can be invaluable. Trust in a tradition or a teacher can bolster our trust in the unfolding of our practice. It can reassure us our efforts are not in vain and that, despite our confusion, we are well oriented on the path.

Regrets

Live long enough and we all entertain certain regrets. We may have recurring thoughts about what could have been or what might not have been, had we done something different than we did. These regrets can hold us back from letting go and moving forward on our path.

We might, for example, cling to thoughts of living a different life, if we had stayed with our ex or left sooner. We might wonder what life would have been like if we'd had children, or if we had switched careers or moved away from home, and so on. We might have done some truly bad things or made some genuinely terrible choices that led to much suffering.

How can we let go of all these regrets?

First, consider the experience of regret as just a repeating thought with an associated emotional response. The emotional response is a bodily sensation, prompting additional cascading thoughts. Try not to put a judgment on these thoughts and sensations. Just see them as they are in the present moment.

Second, consider that whatever you did or didn't do and whatever twist or turn your life took, it really couldn't have happened any other way. You were the person you were when you made those decisions, and you made those decisions according to the thoughts and feelings you had at the time. In other words, the way things happen is unavoidable. If you doubt this, ask yourself if you can know what your next thought will be, or if you can know with certainty what you will do before you do it.

So far, we have just been doing some mental inquiry to provide some perspective, but that may not be adequate to deal with strong regrets. There's one more big layer to this, which is …

Third, accept yourself in your current situation, in this present moment, along with everything that entails, which includes everything you imagine you did or didn't do in the past that led to this current moment. Let the past be the past, and let the future be what it will be. If feelings of regret recur, just return your attention to this fundamental acceptance of yourself and everything in this present moment.

Nostalgia

With regard to our past, nostalgia can also hold us back in our practice. Although in this case the feeling is a positive one, nostalgia still fixes our attention on the past. We dwell in a desire for an imagined golden age to return. Whether we're nostalgic about our youth, some particularly happy period in our adult life, or some era of history, we tend to think if only we could get back to some aspect of that, our life would be better. And this really becomes a distraction from our practice here and now.

Whatever the golden age — be it our childhood, ancient Greece, or the time of the Buddha — it is imaginary. That's the first thing to acknowledge. All golden ages are fantasies, and as fantasies, they are a distraction from the present situation and present practice.

If we lean toward nostalgia, how we imagine our youth is not how things actually were, even if we grant the past a reality in time. The mind distorts past events and emotions to suit its needs and desires. Through nostalgia we amplify the positive, desirable aspects, and mute the negative, undesirable aspects.

Our efforts aren't aided by imagining that the past was more suitable to us or our spiritual practice. We are always here and now. There is nothing more suitable than here and now! We cannot live in the past, nor is the past we imagine real.

Not only is the present moment the most suitable to our practice, it's where practice actually lies. So all these fantasies of other times and golden eras — while sometimes interesting or entertaining — are really distractions from actual practice.

If we find ourselves drifting off into fantasies of the past or making excuses for ourselves based on some golden-age element we lack, we're just putting off our actual practice. Trust me, you are blessed with everything you need, right now. You are blessed beyond imagination! Just bring your attention to the practice at hand, and focus your effort on that.

Fears

Our life experiences and conditioning have left us with many little fears, scattered about the landscape of the ego like a minefield. Every time we wander into and detonate one of these mines, the explosion — big or small — blasts us back into deep egoic consciousness. And in this way, these fears become an obstacle to furthering our practice.

Let's give some examples, so we know the kinds of fears we're talking about. *Nobody really understands me. The world is against me. They're going to think I'm a bad person. What if I say or do the wrong thing? How will I react? What will happen to me? How will I take care of myself? What if something's wrong with me? What if I end up alone? What if my whole life is a failure?* And so on.

These kinds of conditioned, thought-based fears often weave a pattern through our lives. They repeat consistently whenever any similar conditions arise. As soon as they do, we're caught up in a cycle of identifying with the subject of those fears, the ego-self.

Disarming this minefield is part of practice. It's a matter of seeing the process of thought and ego identification clearly. It's a matter of seeing that while some measure of conditioning may always be the background of a body and mind, that's not who or what we really are. It's a matter of getting to know the reality of the Self beyond conditioning.

In the meantime, we still need strategies to deal with these intrusive thought-based fears, because they will continue to arise according to the conditioned pattern and impede our practice in various ways. We need a way to see beyond the cycle of reinforced conditioning.

Even on just the intellectual level, note that these thoughts are not fundamental to your being. They are just thoughts repeated according to conditioning, and they are almost invariably at odds with reality. Notice how little fears can dominate your attention, even when the underlying thoughts are unreal or untrue. Just noting can provide much-needed breathing space in which to continue your practice.

Whenever these fears intrude and become troublesome, take a few breaths to calm yourself down and interrupt the conditioned cascade of responses — the wave of emotions, bodily sensations, and related thoughts. This helps manage the impacts of fear and allows us to accept present thoughts and sensations. Try to look clearly at the fear itself and the cascade of responses. One who sees fear clearly is freed from fear.

Hopes

While the positive aspects of hope can keep us moving forward and shield us from despair and nihilism on the path, it can also become an obstacle. Hopes keep us focused on an imagined future, when things will be better than they are now. Hopes habituate us to putting off happiness in the present moment.

If our practice here and now is to be fully present in our meditation, prayer, or charity, thoughts about a better tomorrow, better you, better situation, better world, and so on, take us out of the essence of our practice. In other words, hopes can be a distraction from the reality of the present.

Likewise, hopes always come with a subtle undercurrent of fear. Between the lines, so to speak, we can discern the fear that our hopes may never come to pass. While we may subconsciously accept these subtle fears as the price for the positive aspects of hope, ultimately they represent an obstacle to clarity.

Lastly, hope can represent a subtle rejection of reality, and that rejection always harbors an element of suffering. What are we really hoping for? Is it not always something other than what actually is, here and now? So our hopes keep us from fully accepting ourselves, our situation, and the world as it really is.

I'm not saying it's useless to consider the future in order to plan and act accordingly. Nor am I entirely discounting the positive — sometimes even necessary — aspects of hope. Hope has its place. But when excessive reliance on hope, indulgent daydreaming or escapism become obstacles, we have to let go of our hopes.

Since thought-based hopes are in some way just the opposite of thought-based fears, we can approach dealing with them in a similar fashion. Again, note that these hopes are essentially just repetitive thought forms relating to an imaginary future. They may or may not be logical or well founded, and they may or may not be useful in terms of planning. So drop these musings about an imaginary future and notice the reality of the present moment.

Whenever these hopes seem to intrude upon your practice or dominate your mind or your mood, take a few deep breaths. Remind yourself that your practice is here and now, your experience is here and now, *you* are here and now, *everything* is here and now.

Loss, Grief, and Anger

Who among us has not experienced loss and grief? It often starts when we're quite young, usually with small things. But as we go through life, the losses and grief come in larger and larger portions: loss of innocence, loss of friends, loss of love, loss of dreams, loss of belief, loss of faith. At some point, it may seem too much to bear, and suppressed or unprocessed grief may arise as despair, anger, or even rage.

In and of themselves, loss, grief, and even rage, are not necessarily obstacles to practice. Although a great hardship to experience, suffering can be a catalyst for inquiry, contemplation, prayer, and other spiritual practice.

Actually, all these various difficulties are like that. On the one hand, they *can* be obstacles and we can feel overwhelmed. On the other hand, our struggles can prompt us to look deeper into our lives, experience, and practice. Ultimately, the very obstacles we struggle with are a catalyst for transformation. But while we seem stuck with our problems, we need helpful strategies to cope with our situation and our suffering.

Grief can feel like a bottomless pit in the heart of your being. Everything is collapsing and being pulled into it. Such grief can feel like a blanket heavier than the universe, a terrible silence that deafens the mind and heart. It's limitless — but a limitlessness experienced through sadness.

The anger that arises through suppressed or unprocessed grief may be projected onto situations or others, which can only increase suffering in this world. But if we catch a glimpse of this anger without projection, it seems to arise from nowhere. The anger doesn't arise from something or someone, but from absence, from that bottomless pit in the heart of our being. For that reason, it can seem inexplicable — a rage coming from nowhere — unless we understand its source as loss itself.

How do we cope with such overwhelming emotions?

There's no trick to make it just vanish from our lives in an instant. But we will fare better if we're honest with ourselves about what we're going through, if we acknowledge our pain and seek to understand our suffering. We should know it's okay to grieve and grieve deeply. It's okay to feel sadness that has no limits. But we have to make space for this process and have faith in it. Grieving can take a long time. We can breathe, accept, and look — that is the work we can do, and that is our practice itself.

My instructions for practice in *That Which is Before You* detail three steps to the practice of processing pain or transforming negative emotions. Those steps are, in short, to focus on breathing, to accept what has happened and is happening now, and to look directly at one's pain, be it physical or emotional. It doesn't have to happen all at once. Big pain can touch our entire lives, the whole of our body and mind, so as necessary, we can approach looking at it in pieces, peeling back the layers as we go. Just do this work, always keeping an eye out for the profound peace that is behind everything.

Boredom

I remember a few martial arts teachers reprimanding students for treating demonstrations or training as if it were entertainment. "I am not an entertainer!" one teacher said. "This is not a show!" another teacher said. Over and over, I received the message that the training you *need* to do is not necessarily the training you *want* to do.

Spiritual practice is much the same, and even more so. The purpose is not to entertain you. And what you want and what you need are rarely the same.

In martial arts, dynamic techniques, movements, or actions can give the appearance of significant training, even when it remains quite shallow. We can entertain ourselves almost indefinitely by keeping the attention on this apparent significance, without ever looking deeply into ourselves, and without ever really learning how to die.

In spiritual practice, there are still novelties and potential entertainments, especially if we constantly change types of practice. But if we stick with a practice, the novelty wears off and ideally isn't fed with too many new variations. The instructions are quite simple, so after just a little practice, we may encounter some measure of boredom.

Take meditation, for example. Basically, you just sit there, so it doesn't take long before most people get a little bored. Is this an obstacle? It can be, if you take boredom as a sign you're doing something wrong or an indication the practice isn't right for you. When that happens, you'll switch practices or add complications to keep the mind entertained. But keeping the mind entertained is not the point. In fact, it's quite the opposite.

As I have already mentioned, asceticism is at the heart of all spiritual practice. The point is to starve the mind of its various entertainments, and to starve the ego of presumed importance. Of course, the mind and the ego don't really care for this. So they protest. *I'm bored,* they say. *This isn't doing anything. This is pointless.*

When I was working in schools, I heard students say all the time that they were bored. "That's great!" I would say. "Boredom is wonderful! Now you can learn how to deal with boredom." And that's the basic strategy when you encounter boredom in practice. It's not a sign you're doing something wrong or need to change anything. It's a sign the practice is working!

Boredom itself and the conflict with yourself over boredom can become an object of direct inquiry. *Who* is bored? *Who* demands to be entertained? What happens if you just sit with this boredom and watch these various thoughts and demands, without being controlled by them. What if you just observe boredom and seek to discover what it really is?

I recently heard a talk by Tulku Jigme Rinpoche, a Tibetan Buddhist teacher, in which he stated quite plainly that "Sadhana [spiritual practice] is not to please you … it is to destroy you." I was immediately struck by how direct this teaching was, and how similar it was to what I had received through martial arts training.

If boredom arises, embrace it! Keep practicing, because now you're really getting somewhere … or nowhere, as the case may be. Now you will have no choice but to face yourself and your internal conflicts. You will have no choice but to start to deconstruct your ego and its various desires, hopes, and fears. Throw everything onto the sacred fire, and you will have no choice but to realize a reality beyond yourself. In short, while boredom may not be the practice you want, it's surely the practice you need.

15

GOING ASTRAY

Q: What is meant by the direct path, and how does that differ from an indirect path?

A: The path is always direct, immediate, present. It is you who wander, the attention caught and the ego reified with each passing thought.

Chasing Experiences

In the course of life and practice, we're likely to have some extraordinary experiences. Whatever the nature of those experiences, we may find ourselves trying to get back there or recapture the feeling, insight, or encounter. Or we may find ourselves always looking for the next big experience, something even more extraordinary. Either way, we're caught in a loop that can be an obstacle.

Sudden insights, manifest bliss, transcendental states, beatific visions, angelic encounters, and other such experiences obviously stand out from the more ordinary experiences of everyday life and practice. Such extraordinary experiences can fill us with wonder, encourage us on the path, and entice us with the promise of deeper mysteries.

It's good to allow such experiences to push us forward, motivate us, and encourage our efforts. But as soon we try to fix an experience in place, recreate an experience, or imagine the next great experience, we're caught in a loop, chasing after a memory or preconceived idea. And while it's fine to allow these experiences to create a sense of wonder and mystery, as soon we start to conceptualize them, fit them into a worldview, or construct a new worldview around them, we're again caught in a loop.

Allow such experiences to be what they are. Be grateful for them, but don't become obsessed by them. Teachings on this subject are quite clear. Such experiences can be significant, but can also become distractions. Don't try to fix in your mind any conceptual understanding of the experience, and don't try to use such experiences as the lynchpins of a worldview.

The experiences are what they are, but you cannot hold onto them and you cannot chase after them. Let go of all particular experiences. From the perspective of consciousness itself, every experience is really the same experience. There is nothing to recreate or chase after. Everything is within you. Just continue with your practice.

Cynicism and Idealism

While I tended to be a bit idealistic, there were times, especially toward the end of my journey, when I turned quite skeptical of anything spiritual. I considered so-called spiritual teachers to be just as lost as anyone, and certainly not enlightened. As I have previously stated, I thought they were all cult leaders, con artists, and deluded dreamers. And while spiritual practice might pass the time or entertain a particular type of person, it certainly wouldn't lead to any sort of truth.

There's nothing wrong with healthy skepticism, but cynicism *can* be an obstacle to practice. Even early on, I ran into this kind of cynicism. After some profound experiences, I delved into spiritual literature and experimented with various practices. And although I was drawn to the idea of enlightenment, there didn't seem to be any way to get there. So, I dismissed it. I thought, *I'm a pretty smart guy and if I can't figure it out, it's probably not real.*

Again, this is definitely an obstacle. In my case, because I didn't really recognize my cynicism for what it was and had no teacher to advise me, it led to twenty more years of wandering in the proverbial wilderness ... and still I had to get through it in the end. But you don't have to wait.

As with all these obstacles, the key is to investigate. Find out who is cynical. What is this cynicism if not just empty thoughts? Who believes these thoughts? What alternative to the truth of reality would you propose? What would such a proposition be, if not just more empty thoughts?

In a way, it's not entirely wrong to at least be skeptical. Usually we just take it too far. We overcorrect. What we should be skeptical about is our own ideas and ideas in general. The Truth is not an idea. As long we search for truth in an idea, that kind of idealism is one obstacle. If, through frustration, we become cynical and dismiss the reality of truth, that is another obstacle. In between these two obstacles is where our practice lies.

Watch the mind and see how it can flip from idealism to cynicism, from one obstacle to the next, and you will see the greater obstacle is the mind itself. If you regard the mind as the source of these obstacles, you're well on your way to overcoming them.

Nihilism

In a quest for truth, logical inquiry and incomplete insight into emptiness can lead the mind into some pretty strange places. Some of those places are desolate realms. The beings who dwell there are haunted by despair and dominated by nihilistic thoughts.

Perhaps, for example, one hears about the emptiness of phenomena, or even has some partial insight into it. The mind is quick to judge and draw conclusions based on incomplete knowledge. That's how we got confused to begin with. So we might think, in a despondent way, *Everything is meaningless and nothing matters.*

Nihilism arises because we hold back to preserve our egos from annihilation. We say, "nothing matters," but we still think *I matter!*

My view matters. Nothing is significant, but *I am significant. I am important.* This schism, this incomplete understanding, is what leads to nihilism, because the self-important ego is left in a realm devoid of meaning.

For perhaps obvious reasons, this can be a serious obstacle. What's the point of practice or effort? What's the point of doing anything, when nothing matters but you? Once caught in such a realm, despair and nihilism become self-reinforcing. It can seem difficult or downright impossible to find our way out.

The most challenging aspect of this obstacle is how strongly we can believe it. Under the spell of nihilistic belief, we don't *want* to make an effort. We don't *want* to get out, which, of course, makes it all the more difficult to overcome.

Getting out is actually quite simple; wanting to get out is the difficult part. Nevertheless, there are two potential exits — one practical and one radical.

The practical way to work with this situation is to engage in meaningful practice for the benefit of others. Since part of the issue is entrenching oneself in a fortress of negative thoughts and feelings, we need to open ourselves to new thoughts and feelings through new experiences. A good direction would be practices on the path of Action, such as charity, community, and service to others.

The radical exit is to fully realize emptiness. To restore balance, everything must be equalized. If we throw *ourselves* into the sea of emptiness, that changes everything. All things being equal again, we are freed from despair and the bondage of nihilistic thoughts.

Beauty, benevolence, love, and meaning arise from the world like never before.

Now, if you're trapped in nihilism, you may think you want the radical way because it sounds easier than serving others. It's *not* easier. It's way more difficult, especially for a person entrenched in nihilism. It's so difficult, in fact, you will need some kind of practice to help. And guess what practice will help blunt your self-importance? It's none other than serving others. So if you find yourself in this nihilistic situation, but still have enough sense to want to get out, of course look into the emptiness of self, but also apply yourself to practice, especially for the benefit of others.

Idolization

When I was a kid, my earliest heroes were fictional characters from movies and comic books. I admired the sincerity and earnestness of Luke Skywalker, the grit and intelligence of Indiana Jones, the charm and ruthlessness of James Bond, and the simplicity and sword-handling of Conan the Barbarian. I was attracted to the world weariness and moral tightropes walked by characters like Mad Max and Rick Deckard.

We could argue the merits of some of these characters as role models, but one thing they all seemed to have in common was a determination to keep going and get the job done! To some extent, these characters still excite and inspire me, although from a more distant perspective. When I was young, there was almost a feeling of wishing I could *be* Indiana Jones. It's a strange desire — a kind confusing impossible sentiment — that inevitably leads to frustration, suffering, and even self-loathing.

There's a big difference between a role model and an idol. In our practice, role models can be very helpful. Whether that person is a living teacher, friend, historical figure, or even a fictional character, a good role model can inspire positive action and earnest practice. Role models inspire us toward our greatest possible potential. But when we idolize someone, we simultaneously want to *be* them and place them so far above us it's impossible to even be *like* them or follow a similar path. So why even try?

In various spiritual traditions, we look to the great teachers, masters, saints, and saviors as examples. But too often we place them on an almost mythical level. They're so far above us we couldn't possibly realize what they realized or do what they did. We turn them into idols, rather than following in their footsteps. This is a big mistake, and inevitably leads to half-hearted practice at best.

None of the great teachers looked down on others. The true guru sees the Self, Buddha nature, and God in all. The guru looks you in the eye and says, "You too are That. You are the supreme reality." The guru does not say you're not good enough, or liberation is not possible. The guru says, "You are a child of God, and liberation is near at hand."

The Buddha did not preach the dharma so we would worship in bondage, but rather so we would practice, inquire within, and awaken as he did. Jesus said, "Ask, and it will be given to you; seek, and you will find; knock, and it will be opened to you." And similar sentiments can be found across traditions. In other words, we're meant to actually walk the path, not to admire it from afar.

Don't let idolization become an obstacle to earnest practice. Demote your idols to role models. Of course, you can't *be* them in the worldly sense, but you can go where they went. Regard the path they took, look where they point, and follow them through practice, with effort and faith, not in an idol, but in the reality of the path. For with this faith, even the impossible is possible.

Predatory Cults

Many people, hungry for spiritual truths and relief from suffering, fall prey to charlatans, grifters, and deluded but charismatic cult leaders. The danger is there. And while we can say the path as a whole is ultimately self correcting, predatory cult membership is a twist best avoided.

I use the phrase "predatory cults" to indicate groups, organizations, or individuals that target and recruit vulnerable people, manipulate them psychologically, control them physically, isolate them socially, fleece them financially, abuse them sexually, and delude them spiritually. Any one or combination of these characteristics can indicate a predatory cult.

Note that not every small, eccentric, or odd-ball spiritual group seeking followers is a predatory cult. Strange or unusual doctrines and teachings do not alone make a predatory cult. We could debate the value of what's being taught in some circles, but there's room on the path for a wide variety of teaching and practices that all fall short of the truth itself.

The use of the word *cult* to denote something sinister is actually fairly recent. In the past, a cult was just a particular religious group. Only recently has it come to mean a type of predatory group engaging in a constellation of harmful and even criminal actions. Such groups use the trappings of spirituality to manipulate, control, and abuse their members, generally for the financial, sexual, and/or egotistic aggrandizement of its leader or leaders.

It's a complex phenomena. The leaders of predatory cults may be cynical charlatans, desperate grifters, deranged psychopaths, or true believers in what they espouse. They can be quite charismatic and convincing. And because spiritual practice *does* involve the potential for transformation and the deconstruction of social and psychological conditioning, seekers might have difficulty discerning what's beneficial and what's harmful. Where do we draw the line?

There are legitimate practices that involve social isolation, for example, but they're taken on voluntarily and not enforced as a control mechanism used to systematically separate and alienate people from family and friends. The difference seems clear when written, but can be difficult to discern for seekers in the midst of seeking.

I can only advise you to trust yourself. You are the ultimate authority, wherever your path leads. If something seems abusive, manipulative, or predatory, walk away. It's far better to throw yourself into the uncertainties of life and the unknowing of confusion than to bind yourself to the illusory certitude of false prophets.

I can assure you with absolute confidence that no person, group, or organization holds a monopoly on the truth. Your path is your path and is not dependent on anybody else. Free yourself of everything, and then see where you stand.

Self Aggrandizement

With some intelligence, a bit of insight, a touch of skill, and a smidge of ambition, we can easily start to think quite highly of ourselves. If you're not already recognized as a great thinker, artist, teacher, or practitioner, surely you deserve to be. And in time, with the work you're doing, surely fame and the admiration of others will come.

The trouble with most obstacles is they start with a bit of genuine experience or observation, but quickly go off the rails as we jump to wild conclusions, expectations, hopes, dreams, desires, and fantasies. Even with a little insight and ability, you're not as smart or perceptive as you think, and your self-aggrandizing assessment of yourself is an obstacle to further development.

It's so obvious when you think about it. How will you realize what is beyond your imagination if you imagine what you know now is so great? Yet people fall into this trap so readily. In fact, they leap into it, more than willing to take quick conclusions over direct inquiry, hope over hard work, fantasies over reality, a puffed-up sense of self over humility, and limited knowledge over the limitless truth.

We're all prone to this a little, because the ego is forever trying to prop itself up and solidify itself and its world. That's just the situation we're dealing with as practitioners. So we have to work from within the situation to overcome obstacles.

Again, I want stress the pattern here. The way to overcome obstacles to practice is *through practice.* The whole purpose of practice is the clarification of obstacles. So we can't take obstacles as an excuse not to practice. It might be a messy, confusing affair, but keep putting forth effort in sincere practice.

Skillful practice, of course, addresses the most prominent obstacles. Where self-aggrandizement is concerned — and its associated negative emotions such as jealousy, frustration, grievance, and cynicism — it's important to practice humility, self-effacement, empathetic joy, loving kindness, and service to others.

Use and develop your intelligence, insight, and skill, of course, but debase your overly-generous view of yourself. You don't have to hate yourself; that's going to too far. Just stop thinking so highly of yourself, that's all. Stop being so proud of yourself. Your intelligence, insight, and skill, whatever they may be, are not your own. Stop taking credit for what little you have received. Just be grateful you've received anything and put whatever you've received to good use in practice.

16

ALL THE OLD PROBLEMS

Q: Why, after so many years of practice, do I still encounter the same difficulties?

A: Your approach is wrong. Stop seeking to solve your problems or get rid of them. Start aiming to transcend them.

Getting Distracted

Distractions are a common challenge when focusing. If you're meditating, the usual instruction is to note the distraction and gently return your awareness to the object of your meditation. In the larger course of life, if we're trying to focus on spiritual practice, the instruction is really the same.

Life has many twists and turns, and the spiritual journey often takes a meandering route. Although, relatively speaking, this may seem like a difficulty, it's perfectly natural and as it should be. There are reasons for our meandering related to the karmic forces at work in our lives. What seems like a distraction may actually be necessary for clarification.

Trust me when I say the spiritual journey is the whole of our lives, exactly as they are. The full course of everything is impossible to fathom.

Even if a year has gone by without practice, or twenty years, judgment is neither necessary nor helpful. Just notice you haven't been practicing, or that you've become distracted by other things, and gently return to your practice. In other words, you can treat spiritual practice as the meditation object for the whole of your life.

Of course, all the advice on dealing with lack of discipline or inconsistent practice applies here as well. Treat consistent practice as a function of habit rather than will power. Build those habits through gentle repetition before pushing yourself with more intensive practice.

When noted in practice, distractions can be helpers, and when abandoned, they strengthen our practice. Don't treat them as the enemy or despair over the wandering nature of your mind and your life. These noted distractions are really your friends, reminding you periodically to get back to your practice, to put forth effort, and to focus on what's important.

Ultimately, distractions aren't an obstacle to the journey, they're a part of the journey. Whatever is happening *is* what's happening, so although we may call some things "distractions," there really aren't any distractions. Likewise, there isn't anything to be distracted from!

Overcoming Doubts

Some skepticism can be an aid on the spiritual journey, helping to ensure we make the effort to go beyond blind belief and dogmatic views. A little skepticism can prompt us toward deeper inquiry and actual experience. A bit of doubt can encourage us to practice in order to find out for ourselves what's real and not real, what's true and not true. But when doubts become so pervasive we become cynical or avoid practice in favor of entertainments and hedonistic desires, then it becomes an obstacle.

Doubts come and go. They're only thoughts. If deep rooted, they repeat until they seem to be something more than thoughts, but they're only thoughts, repeated over and over. In a sense, doubts are just the flip-side of blind belief, and like blind belief, they must eventually be transcended through practice, experience, and insight.

Doubts and beliefs alike come and go throughout our lives. They can be overturned, traded up, and bandied about to suit our tastes, circumstances, and desires. We often think we can overcome doubts and beliefs just by thinking. We argue against our own thoughts. We seek out counter arguments to our thoughts. We think we will overcome our thoughts, but it never really happens this way. It's like trying to clarify muddy water by sweeping it with your hand.

We cannot use the same method to overcome a difficulty that got us into the difficulty to begin with. A knife cannot cut itself, and we cannot think our way out of our thoughts. We will just trade thoughts and views endlessly. We will never really arrive anywhere other than more thoughts and another view. We may think the matter is settled, but eventually we'll start arguing with ourselves again.

So how *can* we overcome our doubts?

Only through clarification ... through actual practice, direct inquiry, insight, and experience. Try to use your doubts as motivation for actual practice. Only by walking the path and doing the work can we really be transformed. We cannot fathom the whole process, and the process cannot unfold any other way than by throwing ourselves into it. We have to surrender to practice, wherever it leads.

Stop trying to sweep the water with your hands. The water has to be left alone, so the mud can settle. The temptation to stick your hands in is so great. You need something else to do, and that's what practice is for.

Strange Experiences

As you progress in your practice, you may experience some very strange things — deep emotions, weird perceptions, and seemingly aberrant mental activity. Experiencing these things without any guidance or reassurance can lead to worries, trepidation, anxiety, and fear. You might even think you're losing your mind.

Of course, mental illness should be addressed, and medical help is available. Nobody should be ashamed to seek out help when needed. This can be a sensitive topic, but I'm not really talking about mental illness or something that's gone wrong. I'm talking about thoughts, sensations, and experiences that can arise when practice actually has its intended effect.

Remember that the purpose of practice is, in some sense, to deconstruct the conditioned mind, dismantle the conditioned view of reality, and break conditioned identification with the body-mind and world. That's putting it a bit bluntly, but when seen in this light, we shouldn't be surprised if we experience some strange and unexpected things along the way.

On the path, I had many remarkable experiences, seemingly good and bad: out-of-body experiences, glimpses of the void, feelings of oneness, feelings of non-self, angelic encounters, alien and demonic encounters, and so on. So many puzzling, wonderful, and terrifying experiences! The neutral, emptied out, dreamlike state prior to awakening can also leave one feeling disconnected or unmoored from reality. Even awakening can leave us wondering if something has gone wrong with our mind, especially since we have essentially transcended the mind and all conditioned views.

Do not fear. If you have persistent torment, thoughts or behaviors that are harmful, potentially harmful, or disruptive to your life or the lives of others, seek out professional help. But if you're merely experiencing some unusual phenomena, even if temporarily scary or unpleasant, it's likely related to tensions between grasping and letting go, between one view and another view, or between all views and total perception. It doesn't necessarily mean you have a problem.

As conditioned views break down and phenomena are seen more clearly, the ego-self will struggle to hang on and reconstruct a view. The resulting tension can give rise to strange, troubling, or even frightening experiences. But there's nothing wrong. There's nothing to be afraid of. If the experience is too much, too soon, or too much all at once, back off your practice a little, lessen the intensity, or even take a break. That's all good.

Seeking advice from a seasoned practitioner or an awakened teacher could be very helpful. We have to be prepared for deeper insight, or what might be progress could turn into setbacks. With regard to practice and experience, there's no time to waste ... but there's also no rush.

Dealing with Demons

The saying about facing your demons exists for a reason. Demons can appear as rage, jealousy, anxiety, fear, nihilism, addiction, and many other powerful negative views and emotions. They can also appear as strange and monstrous forms within meditation, in dreams, in sleep-transition states, or even in everyday life. Whatever the case, don't jump to conclusions about what they are or aren't. However they appear, the important thing in the context of practice is that we endeavor to face them without fear.

The basic approach is no different than processing any perceived negativity. We can start with breathing, acceptance, and direct gazing. It's as simple as that, but dealing with demons is not like dealing with a stubbed toe. It can be an epic struggle and lifelong endeavor. Facing demons takes real courage and often divine aid. It can help to steel our nerves, to take refuge in a higher power, and to set our intention on facing whatever appears, no matter how terrifying.

Like it or not, horror is often a part of the spiritual journey. It is a pilgrimage to the dark, unfathomable, and empty reaches of the soul. In that place, nothing is sacred. The machinations of our hopes and comforts are exposed and disassembled before our eyes. We cannot see this and not be affected. We cannot pass through it and not be changed. Such horror is a reminder that in the end, one way or another, we will face our fears and be transformed.

If you don't know what I'm talking about on some level, you are blessed already … or the demons are still hiding beneath your conscious awareness. Just be aware that one possible difficulty within the context of sincere spiritual practice is the appearance of demons. Try not to panic. I say that, but it's not uncommon to feel overwhelmed, terror-stricken, or otherwise out of control.

Some people will no doubt ask, do you mean *real* demons? Of course I mean real demons! What other sort would require supreme courage and divine aid? But again, don't jump to conclusions about *what* they are. Grasping at conclusions will only lead you deeper into fear and confusion. It's enough that you have to deal with them. Like everything else, demons appear only within consciousness, so don't put all your efforts into imagining what they are, external to you, but rather into facing them.

Symbols, prayers, mantras, and faith can be powerful allies when confronting demons. Don't hesitate to employ them, even if you don't understand their effects. Imagine going into the lair of a powerful vampire. You don't go empty-handed. You carry a crucifix, holy water, litanies against fear, prayers for divine aid, and mantras to steady your nerves. You also need a hammer and some wooden stakes.

All the symbols and prayers are just to aid you in your efforts, to help you face your fears and really look at them, not with hatred, but with compassion for yourself and all beings, even demons. Ultimately, your hammer is not a blunt instrument or a cudgel, but skillful practice, effort, and determination. Your stake is not a weapon; it is the penetrating light of awareness itself. It is love. It is salvation.

Fear!

While we're on the subject of demons, we should say something about fear, because they're closely related. I'm not talking about ordinary everyday thought-based fears, but rather a kind of big fear, an existential fear that can arise in the context of sincere and dedicated practice.

A lot of people encounter this fear or ask about fear, and it was something I encountered on the path, too, which is why I address it, write about it, and talk about it. You might start to think this whole spirituality stuff is pretty scary, though, or assume emptiness or the truth is something frightening. But nothing could be further from reality. I address this fear because it's a very common experience and a common difficulty, *not* because there's anything fundamentally to be afraid of. I have said many times, and I cannot stress it enough, there is nothing to fear.

Fundamentally, there is never anything to fear or worry about. There never has been and there never will be. The truth is wonderful beyond imagination. To know the truth is to know true peace, true safety, true freedom, and true happiness. It dispels fear through the light of awareness. It overcomes all situations and troubles, effortlessly, through all-encompassing love and compassion. But what we're discussing here are difficulties encountered in the context of practice, and fear is definitely one of them.

Of course, place your trust in the higher power and remind yourself there's nothing to fear. Sometimes the mind and body still raise objections, though, and the fear is difficult to let go of. So to manage our fear, we have various practices, prayers, mantras, calming meditations, and so on.

Existential fear can seem like a huge problem, especially when we're deeply identified with some particular idea of our existence. Ultimately, this fear is a paper tiger, but it's very compelling when experienced, so we need some way to work with the associated thoughts and feelings.

The fundamentals are quite consistent. There's no great secret. I have previously explained how to work with and process pain and negativity. The work here is no different. The fundamentals are breathing, acceptance, and direct gazing. Let's review them.

Fear can literally take your breath away. The cessation or disruption of breathing can amplify fear in the body like a feedback loop. You can actually feel paralyzed with fright, so the first thing to tend to is the breath. Focus on breathing. Use breathing to calm the mind and body. With each inhale, breathe into your fear, almost as if you're grabbing hold of it with the breath. Then exhale it out of the body and mind. Do this work to calm yourself down, so you can just be with the sensations of fear without freaking out.

Next is acceptance. Whatever the situation is, it is what it is. Of course, if some action is needed, do that. But either way, what's happening is *already* happening, and your fear has *already* arisen. Just accept it and it's not that bad. So you're afraid. That's okay. So what? There's no shame in it.

Third is direct gazing. Once you've calmed yourself enough to be with and accept your present thoughts and sensations, it's time to really look at them. What is it you're really afraid of? Often we turn away, trying to ignore the actual thoughts and sensations that make up our fear. To the extent you can, look directly at those thoughts and sensations. Just gaze at them. There's no need for judgment or further thoughts. Just see them for what they are.

Once again, all the various difficulties we may encounter in our practice can be dealt with through additional practice. Once you know the fundamentals, you just keep doing this work. Let illumination take care of itself.

17

THE GREAT GATE

Q: What is the greatest obstacle to effective practice?

A: There are really no obstacles whatsoever. Perceived obstacles actually help facilitate effective practice.

The Long Haul

We may wonder how long it will take to reach the end of our practice. We want to look ahead, skip ahead, hope ahead, dream ahead. But everything is always unfolding *now.* It will take what it takes, and when realization dawns it will take no time at all. So while there's no time to waste, there's no rush either. Our practice is always here and now. And true peace is always here and now.

Nothing bars you from awakening except your own interests and attachments, and these karmic forces have already been set in motion. We cannot really go against them. We cannot fight them, we cannot run away, and we cannot wave a magic wand to nullify them. We have to go along with them, see them through, and see through them. Practice helps move this along, all while being a part of those same karmic forces.

In the autumn of our enthusiasm, we may fear commitment. We may wonder if this journey is worth devoting our lives to. We may prevaricate and distract ourselves. But one way or another we have to commit and engage in whatever struggles our path entails. There's no escape. We have to find dedication for clarification, courage for disillusionment, and earnestness for direct inquiry. If we can do that, self-emptying and enlightenment will take care of themselves.

It might take thirty seconds; it might take thirty years. But what matter? Just focus on practice here and now. Whatever happens, you will be better off, and the opportunities for insight and realization never expire.

Remember the principles for engaging in practice: intention, contrast, consistency, inquiry, responsibility, and play. Set your intention on a truth that cannot be overturned, traded, or argued against. Pay attention to contrast as a guide on your path. Practice with consistency to affect real transformation. Apply inquiry from the very beginning. Take responsibility for your practice. And don't take yourself too seriously. However you proceed, only you can do the work. Only you can discover who you really are.

Throw yourself into the process, through the paths of Knowledge, Devotion, Action, and Skill. Your earnestness, effort, and determination are vital for progress. Don't concern yourself with time. Sooner or later you will come to the end of the various causative chains at work in your life. It's inevitable. Because all things come to an end.

Discovering Disillusionment

Although we may have begun our practice with a lot of ideas, desires, hopes, and fears, the real teaching is disillusionment. And the core of practice is always letting go of our ideas, desires, hopes, fears, et cetera. So in the course of our practice, we should not be dismayed or discouraged when we discover some level of disillusionment.

It's all too tempting and easy to stop practicing when disillusionment sets in. When the excitement of our ideas, desires, and hopes — our fantasies — wanes or changes, we often think the fault is with the practice or the tradition. But generally speaking, the practice is working just fine. The fault is with our thoughts and ideas.

Real transformation doesn't happen by confirming our deluded thoughts and ideas, but rather by disillusioning us of them, by freeing us from them. When we begin to get a taste of this disillusionment, it may taste bitter to the grasping mind. The ego wants to cling to its ideas, since it is itself only an idea.

Without your hopes and ideas to cling to, practice may seem dull or uninspiring. Still, keep practicing! Don't let a bit of disillusionment discourage you. It may not feel like it, but this disillusionment is actually a sign of real progress. The slate is being wiped clean. The mind and body are being clarified.

There may be situations in which you must seek out new teachers or additional practices due to some persistent perceived lack or deficiency. That's fine, and to be expected on the journey. It may, for a time, spark new ideas and hopes, or rekindle those that had momentarily been disillusioned. That's fine, too. But keep practicing. A number of practices and teachers may be required before you clarify the various obstacles set in your path and before you exhaust your interest in ideas, hopes, and fantasies. Keep practicing and do whatever is necessary to get to this point. Now the real work can begin.

Until now, you've just been peeling off superficial layers of conditioning. With the ego exposed, exhausted, and disillusioned, we can really start to look deeply and inquire into things more clearly.

The more genuinely disillusioned we become, the deeper our practice can go. Note that the "genuinely" part is key here. An ego that pretends to be disillusioned is just grasping onto a new idea and is still standing in the way of real insight. But as always, when faced with various difficulties, continued effort in practice is the path to clarification. Disillusionment prepares us for the kind of direct inquiry that leads us to the doorstep of awakening.

Letting Go

Practice and the whole spiritual endeavor is a path toward letting go. Although we may learn certain techniques, prayers, or rituals, practice has never been about the acquisition of anything, be it concepts, views, formulations, or experiences. Of course, at times, concepts and experiences are a helpful part of practice, but taken as a whole, practice is a process that guides us toward letting go.

Let's remind ourselves what we're letting go of. It's everything! All concepts and worldviews, all imagined knowledge, past and future, hopes and fears, inside and outside ... and importantly, the compulsive belief in a separate, individual self as the object of our identity.

We don't even really know what it means to let go of all that, until it happens, but nevertheless that's where we're heading. And practice — be it inquiry, prayer, kindness, meditation, or any other sincere spiritual practice — is an aid for getting there. Practice is the boat that takes us across the river of self-centered, limited being. At the far shore, we let go of the boat and pass it on to others in need.

You've heard all this already and are probably aware of the difficulty or even impossibility of willfully letting go. A knife cannot cut itself, and a separate being cannot bring about an end to separation. Any attempt the ego makes only reinforces the duality of perceived independent being.

When it comes to self-emptying, our trust in the process must be complete, because there's nothing more we can do. We can't rely on anything. We must be ready to let go, and just allow what is happening to happen. We drift toward emptiness, okay with being nobody, okay with knowing nothing.

The whole of our practice has led us to this point. From our contact with this life and the teachings, through our enthusiasm for various ideas and activities, through our commitment to find the truth, through our clarification of various obstacles, through our disillusionment with all views, and through our direct inquiry into the nature of self. Finally, it's time to let go, to surrender all and let everything be as it is.

The Great Gate is Wide Open

We are deeply blessed by all those who have gone before us, by all their efforts in practice, by all their suffering and all the things they went through for the sake of peace, happiness, and illumination. We are deeply blessed by all those who came to the end of their path and realized the truth. And we are deeply blessed by all those who have pointed toward it.

There is a kinship among all people, because all are on this journey, whether they know it or not, and because all beings are one being. The smallest kindness and every ounce of effort is of immense significance, because even the most insignificant chain of causation leads to all beings everywhere and to everything throughout all time.

Do not for a second underestimate the gifts we have received. The great spiritual teachings and the awakening they point toward are nothing short of a miracle.

Until enlightenment dawns, take refuge in this great spiritual community, in those realized beings who appear before us, and in the great spiritual teachings. Put forth effort on your own path and in your own practice. Throw out your selfish and deluded hopes, dreams, and ambitions. Cast aside your unfounded fears. Cultivate a sense of selflessness, compassion, and equanimity.

Within spiritual practice, the path is revealed. But we can't merely regard it with admiration. We have to actually walk the path and put the teachings into practice. Only then can we discover for ourselves where the path leads.

May our practice and these teachings benefit all beings, and may they lead you to true peace, true happiness, and true illumination. Do not hesitate to walk toward or into the truth itself. The great gate is wide open.

ABOUT THE AUTHOR

On April 11th, 2016 Matthew Lowes had an unexpected and profound spiritual awakening, just as the great mystics have described. Since this enlightenment dawned, he has endeavored to communicate the insights intrinsic to realization and help others on their spiritual journey. In addition to this work, he continues to be a writer of fiction and games, as well as a student and teacher of martial arts, fitness, and health practices.

matthewlowes.com

Just sit there!

MEDITATION

MATTHEW LOWES

A METHOD FOR THE MADNESS

A complete methodology for meditation practice.

—Coming in 2026

Thank you for reading!

Please post a review online. :)

The next book in this series,
Meditation,
is coming in 2026.

www.ingramcontent.com/pod-product-compliance
Lightning Source LLC
LaVergne TN
LVHW091132080826
845145LV00008B/2128

* 9 7 8 1 9 5 2 0 7 3 0 6 9 *